Biography Today

Profiles of People of Interest to Young Readers

Volume 19
Issue 2
April 2010

Cherie D. Abbey
Managing Editor

Omnigraphics

P.O. Box 31-1640
Detroit, MI 48231-1640

Cherie D. Abbey, *Managing Editor*

Peggy Daniels, Joan Goldsworthy, Jeff Hill, Kevin Hillstrom, Laurie Hillstrom,
Justin Karr, Leslie Karr, and Diane Telgen, *Sketch Writers*

Allison A. Beckett and Mary Butler, *Research Staff*

* * *

Peter E. Ruffner, *Publisher*
Matthew P. Barbour, *Senior Vice President*

* * *

Elizabeth Collins, *Research and Permissions Coordinator*
Kevin M. Hayes, *Operations Manager*
Cherry Stockdale, *Permissions Assistant*

Shirley Amore, Martha Johns, and Kirk Kauffmann, *Administrative Staff*

Special thanks to Frederick G. Ruffner for creating this series.

Copyright © 2010 EBSCO Publishing, Inc.
ISSN 1058-2347 • ISBN 978-0-7808-1059-4

Library of Congress Cataloging-in-Publication Data

The information in this publication was compiled from sources cited and from
sources considered reliable. While every possible effort has been made to ensure reli-
ability, the publisher will not assume liability for damages caused by inaccuracies in
the data, and makes no warranty, express or implied, on the accuracy of the information contained herein.

This book is printed on acid-free paper meeting the ANSI Z39.48 Standard. The infinity
symbol that appears above indicates that the paper in this book meets that standard.

Printed in the United States of America

Contents

Preface 5

Charles Bolden 1946- 9
American Astronaut, Retired United States Marine Corps
Major General, and First African American to Head NASA

Robin Chase 1958- 25
American Entrepreneur and Transportation Innovator,
Founder of Zipcar and GoLoco

Jesse James 1969- 37
American Motorcycle Customizer and Television Personality, Host
of "Monster Garage" and Star of "Jesse James Is a Dead Man"

Chuck Liddell 1969- 51
American Mixed Martial Arts Fighter known as "The Iceman"

Mary Mary
Erica Campbell, Tina Campbell 65
American Gospel Singers and Songwriters, Creators of the Hit
Albums *Thankful* and *The Sound*

Stephenie Meyer 1973- 77
American Author and Creator of the Bestselling Novel Series,
"The Twilight Saga"

Keke Palmer 1993- 93
American Actress, Singer, Star of the Film *Akeelah and the Bee*
and the Television Show "True Jackson, VP"

Paramore
Jeremy Davis, Josh Farro, Zac Farro,
Hayley Williams, Taylor York 105
American Punk-Pop-Rock Band and Creators of *RIOT!* and
brand new eyes

David Protess 1946- 121
American Educator, Legal Activist, Journalist, and Director of
the Medill Innocence Project

Albert Pujols 1980- 139
Dominican-Born American Professional Baseball Player with
the St. Louis Cardinals

Sonia Sotomayor 1954- 155
American Supreme Court Justice and First Hispanic Justice on
the U.S. Supreme Court

Photo and Illustration Credits 173

Cumulative Names Index 175

The *Biography Today* Library 193

Preface

Biography Today is a magazine designed and written for the young reader—ages 9 and above—and covers individuals that librarians and teachers tell us that young people want to know about most: entertainers, athletes, writers, illustrators, cartoonists, and political leaders.

The Plan of the Work

The publication was especially created to appeal to young readers in a format they can enjoy reading and readily understand. Each issue contains approximately 10 sketches arranged alphabetically. Each entry provides at least one picture of the individual profiled, and bold-faced rubrics lead the reader to information on birth, youth, early memories, education, first jobs, marriage and family, career highlights, memorable experiences, hobbies, and honors and awards. Each of the entries ends with a list of easily accessible sources designed to lead the student to further reading on the individual and a current address. Retrospective entries are also included, written to provide a perspective on the individual's entire career.

Biographies are prepared by Omnigraphics editors after extensive research, utilizing the most current materials available. Those sources that are generally available to students appear in the list of further reading at the end of the sketch.

Indexes

Cumulative indexes are an important component of *Biography Today*. Each issue of the *Biography Today* General Series includes a Cumulative Names Index, which comprises all individuals profiled in *Biography Today* since the series began in 1992. In addition, we compile three other indexes: the Cumulative General Index, Places of Birth Index, and Birthday Index. See our web site, www.biographytoday.com, for these three indexes, along with the Names Index. All *Biography Today* indexes are cumulative, including all individuals profiled in both the General Series and the Subject Series.

Our Advisors

This series was reviewed by an Advisory Board comprising librarians, children's literature specialists, and reading instructors to ensure that the concept of this publication—to provide a readable and accessible biographical magazine for young readers—was on target. They evaluated the title as it developed, and their suggestions have proved invaluable. Any errors, however, are ours alone. We'd like to list the Advisory Board members, and to thank them for their efforts.

Our Advisory Board stressed to us that we should not shy away from controversial or unconventional people in our profiles, and we have tried to follow their advice. The Advisory Board also mentioned that the sketches might be useful in reluctant reader and adult literacy programs, and we would value any comments librarians might have about the suitability of our magazine for those purposes.

Your Comments Are Welcome

Our goal is to be accurate and up-to-date, to give young readers information they can learn from and enjoy. Now we want to know what you think. Take a look at this issue of *Biography Today*, on approval. Write or call me with your comments. We want to provide an excellent source of biographical information for young people. Let us know how you think we're doing.

Cherie Abbey
Managing Editor, *Biography Today*
Omnigraphics, Inc.
P.O. Box 31-1640
Detroit, MI 48231-1640
800-234-1340
www.omnigraphics.com
editor@biographytoday.com

Congratulations!

Congratulations to the following individuals and libraries who are receiving a free copy of *Biography Today*, Vol. 19, No. 2, for suggesting people who appear in this issue.

Susannah Chase, Englewood High School, Jacksonville, FL

Judi Chelekis, Vassar Junior/Senior High School, Vassar, MI

Bershard Horton, Longview, TX

Laurie Skien, Bushnell-Prairie City Jr. High School, Bushnell, IL

Judy Yamane, Aliamanu Middle School, Honolulu, HI

Charles Bolden 1946-

American Astronaut and NASA Administrator
Retired United States Marine Corps Major General
First African American to Head NASA

BIRTH

Charles Frank Bolden Jr. was born in Columbia, South Carolina, on August 19, 1946. His father, Charles Frank Bolden Sr., was a social studies teacher and respected high school football coach, and his mother, Ethel M. Bolden, was a librarian, educator, and community leader. He has a younger brother, Warren Maurice Bolden. "Despite long hours and low wages, my parents made the hard choice to remain in public education, motivated by the opportunity to put young students on the path to success," Bolden commented. "They helped launch countless black students toward local, state, and national leadership positions. I was one of them."

YOUTH

When Bolden was growing up in South Carolina, life was very hard for African Americans. Many white people felt a deep and abiding prejudice against black people. African Americans were often treated as inferior, and they were expected to act subservient. During his childhood, segregation—the separation of African Americans and whites—was common in the South. The South was still segregated under what were called "Jim Crow" laws. These laws were founded on the legal principle of "separate but equal," which made it legal to discriminate against African Americans. Jim Crow laws forced the segregation of the races and created "separate but equal" public facilities—housing, schools, transportation, bathrooms, drinking fountains, movie theaters, restaurants, and more—for blacks and whites. Although these separate facilities were called equal, in reality those for blacks were miserably inadequate. African Americans usually attended dilapidated, impoverished schools with underpaid teachers. After leaving school, their opportunities for work were often just as limited.

This was the society in which Bolden was raised. Despite these challenges, he became fascinated at a young age with the nighttime sky and the idea of becoming an astronaut. But he did not think a career in space exploration was possible. "When I was a kid, all astronauts were male, all astronauts were test pilots, all astronauts were white, and all astronauts were the same size," Bolden explained. "I didn't fit into most of these categories." Although his dream seemed out of reach, he grew determined to excel at his chosen path in life and began his journey by dedicating himself to his studies.

EDUCATION

Bolden was an exemplary student and was particularly interested in the subjects of science and math. He was also active in sports, notably swimming and football, and played percussion in the school band. His parents instilled a strong sense of academic discipline in their son. "I was always encouraged to study," he recalled. "I'm very thankful for that now." Demonstrating his ingenuity and persistence, he wrote to his senators and congressmen to express his interest in attending the United States Naval Academy. He also wrote to Vice President Lyndon Johnson, who responded and asked him to contact him again when he was old enough to apply. Despite the challenges of being educated in a segregated school system, he graduated with honors in 1964 from C. A. Johnson High School in Columbia. At Bolden's repeated request, President Johnson arranged for his appointment to the U.S. Naval Academy in Annapolis, Maryland. Bolden was voted president of his class and earned a bachelor's degree in electrical science in 1968. He was one of only four African Americans out of over 800 students to graduate from the academy that year.

Following graduation, Bolden was commissioned as a second lieutenant in the Marine Corps. In 1970 he completed flight training to become a naval aviator. During this time, the United States was involved in the Vietnam War. The U.S. got involved in Vietnam in the late 1950s, when it was essentially a civil war between North Vietnam and South Vietnam. The political makeup of these two countries contributed to the decision by the U.S. to get involved there. It was the Cold War at that time, a period of extreme distrust, suspicion, and hostility between, on the one side, communist countries like the Soviet Union, China, and their allies, and, on the other side, the United States and its allies. North Vietnam was controlled by communists, who wanted to bring their political system to South Vietnam also. Many people in the U.S. felt that it was important to support South Vietnam in order to stop the spread of communism to other nations. In the late 1950s the U.S. began sending in military advisers to help South Vietnam; by the early 1960s, the U.S. began sending in military troops to fight in the war. By the mid to late 1960s, there were strong voices of dissent in the U.S. against American involvement, as President Lyndon Johnson escalated the war and sent hundreds of thousands of soldiers to Vietnam.

> *When Bolden was growing up, he did not think a career in space exploration was possible. "When I was a kid, all astronauts were male, all astronauts were test pilots, all astronauts were white, and all astronauts were the same size," he explained. "I didn't fit into most of these categories."*

After completing his flight training, Bolden was stationed in Thailand from 1972 to 1973. He flew more than 100 combat missions over Vietnam and surrounding areas. Upon returning to the United States, Bolden served as a recruiting officer for the Marine Corps in Los Angeles. He earned a master's degree in systems management from the University of Southern California in 1977, and then attended the United States Naval Test Pilot School at Patuxent River, Maryland, graduating in 1979.

On his first space flight, Bolden is shown at the pilot's station on the Columbia *flight deck prior to re-entry, 1986.*

CAREER HIGHLIGHTS

Bolden's training allowed him to get a job as a test pilot at the Naval Air Test Center's Systems Engineering and Strike Aircraft Test Directorates. He flew various ground-attack test projects before embarking on a long and accomplished career as an astronaut, military officer, and executive.

Joining NASA

During the late 1970s, NASA (the National Aeronautics and Space Administration) began responding to changing attitudes regarding race in America. "As we went through the sixties and through the civil rights movement," Bolden recounted, "NASA realized that it would be untenable for them to have another astronaut selection in the 1970s and 1980s and not include a culturally diverse group of people." He submitted his application to NASA and was admitted into the space shuttle program at the Lyndon B. Johnson Space Center in Houston in 1980. After undergoing rigorous training, he became a qualified astronaut in 1981.

Bolden held a variety of positions with NASA, including special assistant to the director of the Johnson Space Center, technical assistant to the director of flight crew operations, chief of the safety division at Johnson, and lead astronaut for vehicle test and checkout at the Kennedy Space Center in Florida. In addition, he took part in several space flights. The first was the Space Shuttle *Columbia* mission in 1986 (STS-61-C), followed by the Space Shuttle *Discovery* mission in 1990 (STS-31), the Space Shuttle *Atlantis* mission in 1992 (STS-45), and the Space Shuttle *Discovery* mission in 1994, a joint U.S.-Russian space flight (STS-60).

Flights in Space

Bolden's first trip to space, the *Columbia* mission in 1986, involved deploying the SATCOM KU satellite to analyze the effects of microgravity on materials processing, seed germination, and chemical reactions. The crew also conducted experiments concerning protein crystal growth and infrared imaging of Halley's Comet. On the *Discovery* mission in 1990, the crew deployed the powerful Hubble Space Telescope. This telescope, which orbits above the Earth's atmosphere, revolutionized the field of astronomy by providing detailed views of the universe that aren't distorted by the Earth's atmosphere. They also used a variety of cameras, including both the IMAX in cabin and cargo bay cameras, for Earth observations from their record-setting altitude. Bolden served as the pilot on these first two trips to space.

Bolden's third trip to space was the *Atlantis* mission in 1992, for which he served as mission commander. This mission carried part of NASA's Space-

———— **"** ————

"The highlights of any flight always include the spectacular views of the earth," Bolden recalled. "We had some absolutely phenomenal passes over the United States as well as other parts of the world at night. At night you have the opportunity to see all the beautiful lights and the outlines of the cities.... It's really breathtaking."

lab, an orbiting laboratory designed to allow scientists to conduct experiments in a weightless environment. The crew planned to study the sun, the upper reaches of the Earth's atmosphere, and other astronomical objects using a special array of instruments for a series of experiments that constituted ATLAS-1 (Atmospheric Laboratory for Applications and Science). The ATLAS-1 experiments obtained a vast array of detailed measurements of atmospheric properties, including the chemistry of the atmosphere, solar radiation, space plasma physics, and ultraviolet astronomy. These tests contributed significantly to improving scientists' understanding of the Earth's climate and atmosphere.

Bolden's last space flight was the first joint U.S.-Russian mission. Here, five NASA astronauts and a Russian cosmonaut squeeze through the tunnel that connects the space shuttle Discovery *and a module in the payload bay. Mission commander Bolden is upper right; clockwise from Bolden are mission specialists Ronald M. Sega and N. Jan Davis; payload commander Franklin R. Chang-Diaz; mission specialist cosmonaut Sergei Krikalev; and pilot Kenneth S. Reightler Jr.*

In 1992 Bolden was appointed as assistant deputy administrator at NASA headquarters in Washington DC. While in that position, he was selected as commander of the 1994 *Discovery* mission, the first joint U.S.-Russian space expedition. The mission became Bolden's fourth and final space flight. This mission initiated a new era of cooperative efforts in space between the United States and Russia, as Russian cosmonaut Sergei Krikalev joined the STS-60 crew. The shuttle flight was the beginning of an ongoing program in developing the international space station. STS-60 crew members did a range of experiments on the mission, and they also took on the role of teacher as they educate students in the United States and Russia about their mission objectives and what it is like to live and work in space. Bolden later claimed that working with Russian cosmonaut Sergei Krikalev caused him to undergo "a great cultural metamorphosis." He added, "I learned a lot of things from Sergei about operating in space."

After logging more than 680 hours in space, Bolden left NASA to return to military life. He became the deputy commandant of midshipmen at the U.S. Naval Academy in 1994.

Building a Military Career

After returning to active duty in the Marines in 1994, Bolden served as commanding general of 1st Marine Expeditionary Force (I MEF) during Operation Desert Thunder. Mounted in 1998 under President Bill Clinton, Operation Desert Thunder was directed against the President of Iraq, Saddam Hussein. It was part of an attempt to force the government of Iraq to allow the United Nations to inspect the country for signs of weapons of mass destruction. That same year Bolden was promoted to the rank of major general and named deputy commander of U.S. forces in Japan. From 2000 to 2002, he served as commanding general of the 3rd Marine Aircraft Wing at Marine Corps Air Station Miramar in San Diego. In 2002 President George W. Bush nominated him for the position of deputy administrator of NASA. But Bush later withdrew the nomination, opting to "keep key military personnel engaged in the battle against terrorism," according to a NASA announcement. White House spokeswoman Jeanie Mamo explained this decision, stating that Bolden's "expertise and talent is most needed in the Marines."

In 2003 Bolden entered into a new phase of his life and career when he retired from the United States Marine Corps after 34 years of service. His contributions to his country earned him the Defense Superior Service Medal and the Distinguished Flying Cross, among other honors. After his retirement, he reflected upon the difficulties and triumphs of his military career. "As an officer of Marines who happened to be black, I faced some distinct challenges from time to time," he disclosed. "The Marine Corps, however, afforded me opportunities to assume leadership roles and influence the attitudes and actions of Marines and their families, as well as civilians in nearby communities."

After his retirement, Bolden entered into the civilian workforce for the first time in his life. He took high-level jobs at such corporations as American PureTex Water, Marathon Oil, and TechTrans International. He also served as the chief executive officer of JackandPanther LLC, a military and aerospace consulting firm.

Heading NASA

Bolden's highest recognition to date came on May 23, 2009, when President Barack Obama nominated him for the position of NASA administrator, the top position in the organization. He was sworn in on July 17, 2009, becoming the first African American and the second astronaut to head NASA. "It is an honor to have been nominated by President Obama and confirmed by the Senate to lead this great NASA team," he said at his con-

The 1994 launch of the space shuttle Discovery.

firmation. He then outlined his goals for NASA: "We must build on our investment in the International Space Station, accelerate development of our next generation launch systems to enable expansion of human exploration, enhance NASA's capability to study Earth's environment, lead space science to new achievements, continue cutting-edge aeronautics research, support the innovation of American entrepreneurs, and inspire a rising generation of boys and girls to seek careers in science, technology, engineering, and math." The NASA community wholeheartedly embraced Bolden and his vision. "He's a real leader," former Johnson Space Center Director George Abbey told the *Washington Times*. "NASA has been looking for a leader like this that they could have confidence in."

A test of Bolden's leadership came early when he was faced with a difficult financial situation. NASA didn't have sufficient government funding to finance upcoming missions and projects, and he had to figure out how to compensate for the insufficient funding. To remedy the situation, he proposed that NASA seek out privately owned companies to invest in its future. "The government cannot fund everything that we need to do, but we can inspire and open the door for commercial entrepreneurial entities to become involved, to become partners with NASA." He specifically reached out to the African-American business community, encouraging black entrepreneurs to invest in space travel and technology. As he proclaimed in his 2009 address to the Congressional Black Caucus, "We believe that the development of commercial space is a great future frontier of American economic growth. It offers to African-American risk takers, men and women with ideas and the courage to pursue them, a place at the table not just at NASA, but also on the space frontier. That spirit—of risk bringing rewards; of creativity and innovation—is the spirit that America will need now more than ever to strengthen our economy and remain competitive in the global marketplace."

Creating an International Alliance

As part of his ongoing efforts to expand the resources available to NASA, Bolden signed cooperative agreements with a number of countries and organizations. He oversaw pacts with the governments of Canada and France for future space projects designed to study the atmosphere of Mars and survey the surfaces of the Earth's oceans. Similarly, he reached an agreement with the European Space Agency (ESA) regarding cooperation in the field of space transportation. "From shuttle Spacelab missions to the International Space Station, ESA has a long history

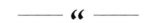

"He's a real leader," former Johnson Space Center Director George Abbey said when Bolden was named NASA administrator. "NASA has been looking for a leader like this that they could have confidence in."

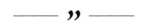

of participating with NASA in human spaceflight," he asserted. "With this agreement, it is our intent to continue to build this relationship, sharing valuable engineering analyses and technology concepts that will help transport humans to low Earth orbit and beyond." He also signed an agreement with the government of Japan, outlining the terms of international collaboration on the Global Precipitation Measurement (GPM) mission, a project to track climate information.

As he lays the groundwork for new NASA projects, Bolden is keeping his eye on future endeavors, especially the possibility of landing on Mars. "In my lifetime, I will be incredibly disappointed if we have not at least reached Mars," he admitted. Another of his future goals is to extend the operation of the international space station beyond its planned closing date of 2016.

Promoting Space Education.

Before Bolden became NASA administrator, he began to notice a lack of enthusiasm from young people about space exploration. "If I go to a classroom today, it's different than when I went as an astronaut in 1980," he explained. "I could ask then, 'How many of you want to be an astronaut?' and every hand went up in the class. When I go to a school today and ask that question, I may see three hands." After his confirmation, he reached out to students in the hopes of promoting interest in NASA. "We can continue to inspire the next generation of NASA scientists and engineers by holding more competitions to help high-school and college students turn their creative talents to exploring our planet, solar system, and galaxy [and] ensuring more government scientists and engineers are mentoring and tutoring in classrooms," he said.

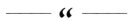

"If you have the ideas, the courage, the hard work, nothing in space is out of reach," Bolden has advised young people. "Don't ever give up on yourself or your dreams. Don't listen to people that tell you what you can't do! If you can dream it, you can do it! I am living proof of that."

To this end, Bolden took the time to meet with students in DEVELOP, a NASA training and development program that brings the concepts of space research to local communities. In addition, he gave an address at the Charles F. Bolden Elementary/Middle School in Beaufort, South Carolina, where he serves as an inspiration in terms of both his accomplishments and his character. The school's principal, Jacque Taton-Saunders, told the *Beaufort Gazette,* "Around the halls of our school, you hear things like, 'We don't do things like that at Bolden,' 'That's not the Bolden way,' or 'Do you think Gen. Bolden got to be an astronaut acting like that?' He's been a great role model."

MARRIAGE AND FAMILY

Bolden is married to Alexis "Jackie" Walker of Columbia, South Carolina. They have known each other since Bolden was three years old, and Bolden

Bolden and NASA Kennedy Space Center Director Bob Cabana welcome home the crew of the space shuttle Endeavour *after they completed a 16-day journey of more than 6.5 million miles.*

has praised her as "a loving and supportive wife who suffered through the difficult periods along with me." Their son Anthony Che was born in 1971 and became a lieutenant general in the Marine Corps. Their daughter Kelly Michelle was born in 1976 and became a plastic surgeon. They have three granddaughters, Mikaley, Kyra, and Talia.

MAJOR INFLUENCES

Bolden has cited Captain Frederick C. Branch as an inspiration on his life and career. The first African-American officer in the U.S. Marine Corps, Branch met Bolden in 1975 at a military convention held in honor of the first black Marines to train at the formerly segregated Montford Point Camp in North Carolina. Bolden has also named Frank Peterson—the first African-American aviator in the Marine Corps and the first black Marine to be promoted to the rank of lieutenant general—as a source of inspiration. Bolden has acknowledged the strength that he has drawn from such leaders. "Though my 34-year journey as an active duty Marine Corps officer was not without its challenges, I was blessed with the legacy of strong and dynamic men."

Bolden has also credited the pioneers of the civil rights movement with paving the way for his successes by fighting against the odds, and he has

Bolden with Anatoly Perminov, the head of the Russian Federal Space Agency, shown at the Mission Control Center in Russia.

consistently tried to spread that spirit of bold accomplishment to subsequent generations. "Believe in yourself," he urged in J. Alfred Phelps's book *They Had a Dream*. "Don't let anybody else determine what your life is going to be. Pick some goal that's just slightly out of your reach, then go for it. Be persistent and don't be afraid of failing. Some of my best accomplishments … have come after I've failed, picked myself up, and tried again." By demonstrating this sense of determination and dedication, Bolden has become a role model himself. "If you have the ideas, the courage, the hard work, nothing in space is out of reach," he has advised young people. "Don't ever give up on yourself or your dreams. Don't listen to people that tell you what you can't do! If you can dream it, you can do it! I am living proof of that." As Senator Lindsey Graham declared in an interview, "There's no better example of what we can do in America than what General Bolden has achieved."

MEMORABLE EXPERIENCES

During his four space missions, Bolden saw many sights that he will never forget. "The highlights of any flight always include the spectacular views of the earth," he recalled. "We had some absolutely phenomenal passes over the United States as well as other parts of the world at night. At night you have the opportunity to see all the beautiful lights and the outlines of the cities…. Down south towards Antarctica you would frequently see what they call the 'southern lights'; the Aurora Australis," he explained. "The lights are caused by electrically charged particles coming into the atmosphere from outer space and causing energy to be given off in the form of light…. It's really breathtaking."

In contrast to the awe-inspiring beauty and thrill of space travel, an astronaut's job also encompasses great risks. The dangers associated with his career, however, have never deterred Bolden. When the Space Shuttle *Columbia* tragically exploded over Texas in 2003, he mourned the loss of his colleagues but remained unshaken in his dedication to space flight. "Why would I do something different when I've been blessed with a life like I've had," he explained. The *Columbia* tragedy also served as a reminder of the destruction of the Space Shuttle *Challenger*, which exploded shortly after take-off in 1986. "Every time I watch a launch, even today, [the *Challenger*] is on my mind," he confessed. Remaining committed to the shuttle program despite such concerns served to strengthen his legacy as an astronaut.

"Believe in yourself. Don't let anybody else determine what your life is going to be. Pick some goal that's just slightly out of your reach, then go for it. Be persistent and don't be afraid of failing. Some of my best accomplishments … have come after I've failed, picked myself up, and tried again."

Bolden's accomplishments as a marine and an astronaut were recognized by his home state in 1999 when he was inducted into the South Carolina Hall of Fame. During the induction ceremony, he urged a crowd of local schoolchildren to follow in his footsteps. "Do the best you can and dream big dreams," he advised. "A dreamer, that's what I was, what I am, and what our youth should be." In 2006 he was honored for his NASA career by being inducted into the Kennedy Space Center's U.S. Astronaut Hall of Fame in Florida.

HOBBIES AND OTHER INTERESTS

When he is not involved with his daily duties as NASA administrator, Bolden enjoys such sports as soccer and racquetball, and keeps in shape by running and swimming. He is also an active member of the Marine Corps

Association, the University of Southern California Alumni Association, and the Naval Academy Alumni Association.

HONORS AND AWARDS

University of Southern California Outstanding Alumni Award: 1982
National Technical Association Honorary Fellow: 1983
Defense Superior Service Medal: 1986
NASA Space Flight Medal: 1986; 1991; 1992; 1994
NASA Exceptional Service Medal: 1988; 1989; 1991
University of Southern California Alumni Award of Merit: 1989
Defense Meritorious Service Medal: 1990
AAS (American Astronautical Society) Flight Achievement Award: 1991
NASA Outstanding Leadership Medal: 1992
NASA Distinguished Service Medal: 1993; 1995
Yuri A. Gagarin Gold Medal: 1995
Inducted into the South Carolina Hall of Fame: 1999
Inducted into the Kennedy Space Center's U.S. Astronaut Hall of Fame: 2006

FURTHER READING

Books

Encyclopedia Britannica, 2009
Gubert, Betty Kaplan, Miriam Saywer, and Caroline M. Fannin. *Distinguished African Americans in Aviation and Space Science,* 2002
Phelps, J. Alfred. *They Had a Dream: The Story of African-American Astronauts,* 1994
Walton, Darwin McBeth. *Overcoming Challenges: The Life of Charles F. Bolden, Jr.,* 1999 (juvenile)
Who's Who among African Americans, 16th ed., 2003

Periodicals

Jet, Feb. 21, 1994, p.9
New York Times, Mar. 3, 1986, p.9; May 16, 2009, p.A11
Washington Post, Feb. 3, 2003, p.C1
Washington Times, May 24, 2009, p.A1; July 20, 2009, p.E7

Online Articles

http://www.news.cnet.com
  (CNET, "Obama Picks Former Astronaut to Lead NASA," May 23, 2009)
http://www.jsc.nasa.gov/Bios/htmlbios/bolden-cf.html
  (NASA, Lyndon B. Johnson Space Center, "Astronaut Biography:

Charles Bolden, Major General, USMC Ret., NASA Administrator," Sep. 2009)

http://topics.nytimes.com/topics/reference/timestopics/people/b/charles_f
_bolden_jr/index.html
(New York Times, "Times Topics: Charles Bolden," multiple articles, various dates)

http://www.time.com
(Time Magazine, "Charles Bolden: The Next Boss at NASA?" May 19, 2009)

ADDRESS

Charles Bolden
NASA Headquarters
300 E St. SW
Washington, DC 20546-0001

WORLD WIDE WEB SITES

http://www.nasa.gov/audience/forstudents
http://www.jsc.nasa.gov/Bios/htmlbios/bolden-cf.html
http://raahistory.com
http://www.nasm.si.edu/blackwings

Robin Chase 1958-

American Entrepreneur and Transportation Innovator
Founder of Carsharing Company Zipcar and
Ridesharing Network GoLoco

EARLY YEARS

Robin Maria Chase was born on September 19, 1958, in The
Hague, Netherlands. The Hague is the third largest city in the
Netherlands. Although it is not the nation's capital city, The
Hague is the center of the Netherlands government. Her
mother, Shirley Gustafson Chase, was a physical therapist and
an artist. Her father, Robert W. Chase, was a U.S. Foreign Service officer who held diplomatic posts in many international

Robin as a baby with her mother.

cities. At the time of Robin's birth, her father was posted in Beirut, Lebanon. There was an outbreak of civil war, and the family was evacuated. Her mother decided to go to The Hague, which she knew would be safe. Robin has five siblings: Linwood, Kristenna, Ragnar, Ruth, and Mark.

Chase grew up all over the world. Her family moved a lot when she was growing up, depending on where her father's work required him to live. They spent time in many different cities, including Alexandria, Virginia; Alexandria, Egypt; Beirut, Lebanon; Damascus, Syria; Jeddah, Saudi Arabia; Jerusalem, Israel; Mbabane, Swaziland; and Tangier, Morocco.

Chase attended college in the United States. She graduated from Wellesley College in 1980 with a Bachelor of Arts degree (BA) in English, French, and philosophy. She then attended the Massachusetts Institute of Technology (MIT) Sloan School of Management, where she earned a Master of Business Administration degree (MBA) in 1986.

MAJOR ACCOMPLISHMENTS

Robin Chase has created unique new transportation programs that help people arrange carpools, share rides, and rent cars in small blocks of time instead of by the day. Chase works to help people become less dependent on personally owned cars, both to save money and to reduce the amount of pollution produced by cars.

Chase has always been interested in creative problem-solving. After graduating from Wellesley, Chase worked for various nonprofit organizations. During this time, she realized that many of these organizations needed people with business management skills in order to successfully bring their innovative ideas to life. This need inspired Chase to enroll in graduate school at MIT, where she first became interested in the many ways that transportation problems can influence people's lives. The need for reliable, affordable transportation can affect people's choices about where they live, where they work or go to school, and how far and how often they can travel to the other places they need to go.

Chase began to see that typical American transportation habits were inefficient and wasteful—with most people owning their own car and driving alone most of the time. She saw a few big problems with the American system of individual car ownership. First, it results in a much larger number of vehicles on the road every day than are strictly necessary. All of these cars use a large amount of gas and oil and produce too much pollution and traffic congestion, particularly in cities. Second, having a car isn't a good solution for everyone because of the high cost of owning, operating, and maintaining a car. But some people need a car to get to work or school, and public transportation doesn't serve every community. And individual car ownership is a fundamental part of modern American culture. Chase wanted to change people's attitudes about car ownership and get people to consider other options—both for their own personal benefit and to reduce the environmental impact of overcrowded highways.

Chase thought that if people understood the real cost of owning and driving a car, they might be more open to new ideas. "If everyone really understood and paid for the cost of each car trip, we would likely sometimes choose another more efficient way to travel: by foot, by bike, subway, bus, or train." With individual car ownership, each car owner bears the full burden of paying for the car, insurance, maintenance, repairs, gas, and sometimes parking fees. "According to the National Households Consumer Survey, across the nation it costs $24 per day on average that people are spending in America on their car, day in and day out," Chase explained. "If I were to tell you that it was going to cost $125 a week to go to work, you would say, no way, I'm not going to do it. But we are doing it—we just don't realize we're doing it."

> ❝
>
> *"If everyone really understood and paid for the cost of each car trip, we would likely sometimes choose another more efficient way to travel: by foot, by bike, subway, bus, or train."*
>
> ❞

Developing a Big Idea: Zipcar

By 1999, Chase was working on an idea for a community carsharing system based on similar programs common in European cities. The idea came partly from her own need for part-time access to a car, and she thought there would be others with a similar need. "This is what I wanted personally. I have three kids and one car that my husband takes to an office where it sits, unused, for eight hours a day, so I never have access to a car.

Zipcar members have access to a wide array of vehicles, allowing them to use different types of vehicles for different situations.

Plus, I live in a city and there's no way ... I want to have a second car that I have to maintain and own and park. The lightbulb went off: the costs for car ownership definitely outweigh the benefits for me in the city, and wireless and the Internet can make this easy."

Some people were initially skeptical that Chase's carsharing idea would work. Would Americans willingly give up their own cars in order to share a car with strangers? She thought they would, once they understood the benefits and how easy it would be to use her program. However, initial research with potential carsharing users revealed that many people didn't like the idea of sharing. "Forty percent of the people I talked to had an extremely negative reaction to the word 'sharing,' Chase recalled. "The word makes people nervous. They feel they're being scolded or told to wait their turn. At one point I banned my staff from using the phrase 'car sharing.' Do we call hotels 'bed sharing'? That's way too intimate. Do we call bowling 'shoe sharing'? Who would want to bowl?"

After thinking for a long time about how to convince reluctant potential customers to give her idea a try, Chase chose to name her new program Zipcar. She thought the name conveyed the sense that car sharing was a fun new way of getting around, without all the hassles and expense of car ownership. "I wanted people to feel that they were the smart ones, the cool, hip, urban insiders who figured out that to live in a city and to own a car was stupid." By January 2000, Chase had officially founded Zipcar with business partner Antje Danielson.

The Zipcar plan combined Internet and wireless technology to create what Chase envisioned as "the perfect web application—creating an online community to share a common resource." Wireless technology was new at that time and was only really being used for mobile phones. Chase saw the potential for so much more. "I thought,'Wow, this is what the Internet was made for: sharing a scarce resource among many people. This is what wireless was made for: we can make transactions very easy for end users and brokering those transactions will cost us next to nothing."

Zipcar has revolutionized the way that people use cars. Instead of owning their own car and paying all of the associated costs, Zipcar members

"It costs $24 per day on average that people are spending in America on their car, day in and day out," Chase explained. *"If I were to tell you that it was going to cost $125 a week to go to work, you would say, no way, I'm not going to do it. But we are doing it—we just don't realize we're doing it."*

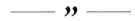

have on-demand access to a car and pay only when they need to use it. Cars are parked in various locations, usually near high-traffic areas or public transportation stops. Members use Zipcar's web site (www.zipcar.com) to reserve a car for any amount of time they need. A special wireless-enabled keycard is coded with the individual member's information and is used to unlock the car at the reserved time. The amount of time and mileage per trip is recorded and transmitted wirelessly to Zipcar's database, and members' accounts are automatically charged at the end of each trip. Many Zipcar members find the service more convenient than public transportation and cheaper than a taxi or a traditional rental car.

Zipcar Grows Rapidly

Zipcar launched in Boston, Massachusetts, with a single lime green Volkswagen Beetle. More cars were added as membership grew quickly in the first few months, with an average of 25 new members joining the service each week. The company continued to grow by leaps and bounds during

The Zipcar iPhone app is a perfect example of Chase's interest in both transportation and technology.

its early years. As word of the new service spread, Zipcar swelled to more than 800 members in the Boston area within its first year. Zipcar began operating in Washington DC in 2001 and New York City in early 2002. Soon other cities were added in the U.S., Canada, and Europe. Businesses and government agencies began to replace their vehicle fleets with Zipcar contracts. "When you share a car, it's great for companies, great for individuals, great for cities," Chase explained.

But the rapid growth was unexpected and nearly overwhelmed the small company. "You have your brilliant idea, and you have your future vision, but you can't anticipate the path immediately in front of you. And it's a good thing you can't, because if you could, you would be too tired to start," Chase recalled. "There were moments when I had serious second thoughts, but it was too late. I never expected there would be a point when there was no turning back." By 2009, Zipcar was maintaining a fleet of more than 6,500 vehicles serving more than 350,000 individual members. Research has shown that every Zipcar is responsible for a reduction in private car ownership of eight to ten vehicles. "The environmental piece of it was obvious," Chase stressed. "I don't think I would have started a business that had no social benefits because I wasn't interested in spending 120 hours a week for years doing something that was just to make money."

In 2003, Chase stepped down as Chief Executive Officer (CEO) of Zipcar. Soon after, she won the competitive Loeb Fellowship from the Harvard University Graduate School of Design for 2004-2005. The fellowship is awarded to people working to improve the built environment—meaning, all the parts of the world that have been constructed by humans. Chase decided to use the fellowship to study transportation policy, urban design, and city planning. "My experience with Zipcar illuminated for me the tight links between how we build our cities, the resulting mobility options, and our ability to curb CO2 emissions," she explained. "Think about how we built out the national highway interstate network in the '50s. We built highways, we ripped out all the trolleys, and we didn't build any trains. We created our destiny as a car-dependent nation because that's the infrastructure we built up.... We built our houses on one-acre lots and now our choices for interaction are defined by that." At Harvard, Chase focused her work on reducing the environmental impact of personal transportation. "How can we reduce CO2 emissions in a world in love with the car and with a built environment that is totally dependent on it?"

After completing the fellowship, Chase founded the Meadow Networks consulting firm. Meadow Networks advises governments and businesses about wireless applications for transportation and the many ways in which innovative approaches to transportation can help communities grow and thrive.

> ———— " ————
>
> *"My experience with Zipcar illuminated for me the tight links between how we build our cities, the resulting mobility options, and our ability to curb CO$_2$ emissions," Chase explained. "Think about how we built out the national highway interstate network in the '50s. We built highways, we ripped out all the trolleys, and we didn't build any trains. We created our destiny as a car-dependent nation because that's the infrastructure we built up."*
>
> ———— " ————

Beyond Carsharing: GoLoco

In 2007, Chase founded GoLoco, the world's first organization that combines social networking, ridesharing (also known as carpooling), and online payment. Chase chose the name to convey the flexibility and freedom of cooperative transportation. She explained, "GoLoco: It means go *loco*— go crazy, go free-spirited. Go location to location with local transportation. Go low cost. Go low carbon dioxide."

Chase envisioned GoLoco as a natural extension of the Zipcar service. "Carsharing only works in dense metropolitan areas or in cases where people don't need a car to get to work. If you need a car to get to work, you're going to have to own your own car. The cost of carsharing is too high for a daily commute.... That's why I did GoLoco—I said, what about all those other people who are feeling similar transportation and mobility pains but they need a car to get to work? Ride sharing is for those people." Chase designed GoLoco to help people improve their own quality of life while helping the environment. "I see GoLoco as an immediate solution. It means I don't have to wait for the government to introduce carbon taxes or congestion charges, or put in smart development or light rail or transit. Today, with the infrastructure we have, we can do something which dramatically reduces costs and emissions."

——— **"** ———

"My goal is to reshape the way people feel about car ownership," Chase declared. "I think when we look back at ourselves sitting alone in our 120 square feet of car, driving down these highways with incredible storage costs and incredible operating costs, I think we will look back at how we travel today and just be astounded: astounded at the cost, astounded at the waste."

GoLoco helps people quickly set up shared car trips using concepts of social networking. Members create a profile for themselves and can invite or add friends, neighbors, coworkers, classmates, or anyone else to their personal group. Members post requests for trips they want to share, and other members respond to join the trip. "Think about standing in a mall, looking at a parking lot," Chase said in explaining the basic idea of GoLoco. "You know that a large number of people there are going exactly where you're going in the next five minutes." GoLoco members use the service to carpool to the mall or any other destination, instead of driving separately. The social networking function allows GoLoco members to choose to re-

——— **"** ———

strict access to their posted trip requests to only those people in their group. In this way, members can feel safer about arranging trips with trusted friends or acquaintances rather than with strangers.

The GoLoco web site also handles online payment transactions, making it easy for people to share the cost of a car trip. Chase wanted to include online payments in the GoLoco service to help people avoid any awkwardness about asking for or accepting payment from friends and to make it extremely easy to use the service. Passengers pay the driver for part of the

Chase continues to explore new ideas about transportation and technology.

cost of the trip, which is agreed upon in advance. If there is one passenger, they pay the driver for half the cost of the trip. If there are two passengers, each one will pay the driver one third the cost of the trip. Payments are automatically transferred from passenger accounts to the driver's account. GoLoco users like the system because it is easier than trying to handle cash and make change during a trip.

Creating Change

Chase's work to pioneer new ideas and methods of transportation has earned praise and recognition from the environmental and business communities alike. *Time* magazine called her work an illustration of the best use of the Internet, saying her ideas are "not well-intentioned yet futile do-goodism but business that's also a community service. It's about people using the Internet to work together in the service of one another." She has been recognized as an international transportation expert known for having big ideas and the skills to bring her ideas to life. "My secret was just believing that the world could be the place I wanted it to be," Chase said. "Small actions add up to big actions. And we can't get to the big results without all the small ones on the way."

"My goal is to reshape the way people feel about car ownership," Chase declared. "I think when we look back at ourselves sitting alone in our 120 square feet of car, driving down these highways with incredible storage costs and incredible operating costs, I think we will look back at how we travel today and just be astounded: astounded at the cost, astounded at the waste. It's such a wacky idea that we'd want to be alone in our cars spending huge sums of money and all that parking space, when it was less fun and more expensive and kind of crazy."

HOME AND FAMILY

Chase lives in Cambridge, Massachusets, with her husband, Roy Russell. They have three children.

HONORS AND AWARDS

100 Hottest Ideas List (*Fortune Small Business*): 2001, for Zipcar
100 Hottest Technology Ideas (*CIO*): 2001, for Zipcar
Top 100 Innovators (*InfoWorld*): 2001
Fast 50 Champions of Innovation (*Fast Company*): 2002
Start-Up Woman of the Year (Women's Business Hall of Fame): 2002
Alternative Transportation Innovator of the Year (AltWheels Transportation Festival): 2003
Governor's Award for Entrepreneurial Spirit (Massachusetts): 2003
Small Business Excellence in Customer Service Award (Dell/National Federation of Independent Business): 2004, for Zipcar
Entreprenuer of the Year (Ernst & Young): 2005
Top 35 Travel Innovators (*Travel & Leisure*): 2006
Top 10 Designers (*BusinessWeek*): 2007
Time 100 Most Influential (*Time*): 2009

FURTHER READING

Periodicals

Boston Globe, Apr. 23, 2007
Boston Globe Sunday Magazine, Nov. 18, 2007
Business Week, Aug. 13, 2007
New York Times, Mar. 1, 2002; Sep. 2, 2007; Mar. 3, 2009
Time, Apr. 30, 2009; Sep. 24, 2009

Online Articles

http://www.boston.com/business/articles/2007/04/23/carpooling_gets
_a_new_dash_of_green
(Boston Globe, "Carpooling Gets a New Dash of Green," Apr. 23, 2007)

http://www.boston.com/bostonglobe/magazine/articles/2007/11/18/earth
_angels_the_entrepreneur
(Boston Globe Sunday Magazine, "Earth Angels: The Entrepreneur,"
Nov. 18, 2007)
http://www.businessweek.com
(Business Week, "Share a Car, Save the World," Aug. 13, 2007)
http://www.nytimes.com/2002/03/01/automobiles/may-i-borrow-the-car
-new-service-says-yes.html
(New York Times, "May I Borrow the Car? New Service Says Yes," Mar. 1,
2002)
http://www.nytimes.com/2007/09/02/automobiles/02LOCO.html
(New York Times, "Thumbing Rides Online," Sep. 2, 2007)
http://www.nytimes.com/2009/03/08/magazine/08Zipcar-t.html
(New York Times Magazine, "Share My Ride," Mar. 8, 2009)
http://www.oswego.edu/news/index.php/site/news_story/it_all_matters
(State University of New York at Oswego, "It All Matters," May 16, 2009)
http://www.time.com/time/specials/packages/completelist/0,29569,189441
0,00.html
(Time, "The 2009 Time 100: Robin Chase," Apr. 30, 2009)
http://www.time.com/time/specials/packages/article/0,28804,1898067_192
6040_1926049,00.html
(Time, "Time 100 Roundtables," Sep. 24, 2009)
http://urbanomnibus.net
(Urban Omnibus, "A Conversation with Robin Chase," June 10, 2009)

ADDRESS

Robin Chase
GoLoco
40 Cottage Street
Cambridge, MA 02139

WORLD WIDE WEB SITES

http://www.robinchase.org
http://www.meadownetworks.com/?page_id=3

Jesse James 1969-

American Motorcycle Customizer and Television
Personality
Founder and CEO of West Coast Choppers
Host of "Monster Garage" and Star of "Jesse James
Is a Dead Man"

BIRTH

Jesse Gregory James was born on April 19, 1969, in Lynwood,
California. He grew up in the same area, in various homes
around Compton and Long Beach. His father, Larry James,
made his living selling antiques and used furniture at flea

markets. His mother worked as a florist. He is named after Jesse James, the famous American bandit who was gunned down in 1882. James's great-great-grandfather was a cousin of the outlaw.

YOUTH

James's parents split up when he was five years old, and Jesse lived with his father after that. Larry James has said that even at a very young age, his son had the interests and skills that would eventually make him famous as a motorcycle customizer. "It didn't matter if it was Legos, a pile of Tonka trucks, or his bikes," his father once recalled, "you could always find Jesse with everything laid out on the floor, tearing things apart to see if he could make them better in some way."

> "It didn't matter if it was Legos, a pile of Tonka trucks, or his bikes," his father once recalled, "you could always find Jesse with everything laid out on the floor, tearing things apart to see if he could make them better in some way."

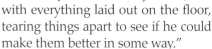

For a while, Larry James's shop was located next door to Performance Machine, owned by Perry Sands. The company made aftermarket accessories for motorcycles—special parts that owners of mass-produced bikes can add to their machines to give them some individual style. Performance Machine was filled with men and noisy equipment, changing pieces of metal into motorcycle parts. James loved to watch them. "My early, early memories are going next door and playing with all the metal chips, and seeing those guys," he recalled. "I don't even remember the inside of my dad's shop, but I can remember what it looked like inside Perry's shop."

James was seven years old when he got his first motorcycle, a Kawasaki 50 cc minibike that he rode every day. When he was about 12 years old, he began learning the art of welding and started his first serious customizing project. Taking an old, beat-up Schwinn bicycle from the 1940s, he cleaned it up, repaired it, and tricked it out with lots of chrome and a great-looking pinstripe paint job. His creation sold at a flea market for $850. The experience taught James that both personal satisfaction and financial rewards could come from working with his hands.

James showed a real flair for learning about machines and metal, but he also had a knack for getting into trouble. He was left on his own a lot, and he got involved in illegal activities, including car theft. On three occasions, he was taken into custody by the California Youth Authority, which deals with young lawbreakers. James eventually changed his ways when he realized that if he didn't, he would end up in the "big-boy jail," as he put it.

EARLY MEMORIES

James has been fascinated by motorcycles since he was very young. "I remember seeing a pack of [the motorcycle club] Hell's Angels blasting by our family car when I was about six, and they were all riding choppers," he recalled. "I remember all the noise and all the chrome. It was the coolest thing I ever saw. I knew then that I was going to be involved in motorcycles in some way."

EDUCATION

James didn't have an easy time at school. He played on the high school football team, but was frequently kicked out of practice for being too rough. A loner at school, he said that "I hated everybody and everybody hated me." Those feelings of being at odds with everything and everyone inspired his first major motorcycle project. He decided to build a "big, loud obnoxious bike … to make'em hate me more." He had very little money to work with, but he succeeded in putting together a rigid-framed, stripped-down, no-frills chopper. His finished ride was definitely loud and fast, and he had done all the work on the frame, engine, and paint job himself.

After graduating from La Sierra High School in Long Beach, James began studying at University of California, Riverside, where he had been awarded a football scholarship. A knee injury ended his athletic career, however. He left college before completing his degree.

FIRST JOBS

After building that first chopper in high school, James continued working on new motorcycle projects, using a corner of his mom's garage as his shop. In 1988, when he was 19 years old, he came up with a name and logo for the business he dreamed of owning. It was "West Coast Choppers," with the name incorporated into a Maltese cross design. Even at that age, he was shrewd when it came to marketing. He knew it would be important to his success to have a brand with strong appeal. He printed up about ten T-shirts featuring the logo and tried to give them to his friends, saying: "Trust me, this is my shop." Their response, he recalled, was generally something like: "You don't have a shop. What are you talkin' about?" Most of them didn't even want the free shirt. Despite their skepticism, James said: "I always knew that West Coast Choppers was gonna be it.

A chopper designed and built by James and his team.

That was my dream." He continued to use his original logo as his business slowly took shape and prospered, and millions of people all over the world now wear West Coast Choppers T-shirts.

James knew it would take money to realize his dream of owning a motorcycle shop. He had matured into an imposing man, over six feet tall with lots of muscle. After taking some specialized training, he found work as a professional bodyguard. In that capacity, he provided security for musical acts ranging from the pop star Tiffany to heavy-metal bands like Slayer, Danzig, and Soundgarden. Working in security paid well, and when he wasn't on tour he was able to keep working on motorcycles. After about five years on the job, however, while working at a concert in Detroit, he suffered a dislocated elbow—a very painful injury. The incident helped him decide it was time to get out of the bodyguard business and pursue the West Coast Choppers dream full-time. In 1992, his shop was officially launched.

Working at Many Apprenticeships

James had some very clear ideas about how he wanted to do things at West Coast Choppers. He knew he didn't want to take out any loans; the business should pay for itself. He wanted everything from his shop to be a product of great design and craftsmanship. He hoped to eventually manufacture most of the parts for his motorcycles on-site, rather than buying parts elsewhere. James understood that he had a lot to learn before he could reach these goals and that it would take many hours of hard work to reach the level of quality he wanted. He set out on a series of apprenticeships under the masters of metalworking and machine-building.

James started at Performance Machine, the same shop that had fascinated him as a little kid. Owner Perry Sands first assigned him to the research and development department, and later allowed him to design and build the prototype Corbin Warbird body kit. Sands appreciated James's natural talent and his hard-working attitude. After about a year and a half, James moved on to work with Boyd Coddington, a legendary car customizer. Serving as a design and fabrication specialist at Coddington's shop, James improved his ability to transform ideas and sketches into working parts. He also mastered the operation of the computer numerical control (CNC) machine. The CNC can read any three-dimensional design programmed into it and then

"I remember seeing a pack of [the motorcycle club] Hell's Angels blasting by our family car when I was about six, and they were all riding choppers," James recalled. *"I remember all the noise and all the chrome. It was the coolest thing I ever saw. I knew then that I was going to be involved in motorcycles in some way."*

create that shape out of metal. The machine is very important in the world of custom cars and motorcycles, particularly for producing wheels. Leaving Coddington's shop, James next worked with Ron Simms, another well-known customizer in the San Francisco area, who taught him a lot about producing fenders and other sheet-metal accessories.

One thing James had noticed about many older choppers he'd worked on was the way their parts were fabricated with cheap materials and substandard techniques. Welds that separate and parts that break can cause accidents, and on a fast-moving chopper an accident can easily be fatal. James wanted his creations to be really rugged, able to hold up to the toughest conditions. His desire to learn the best possible working methods led him to the East Coast in 1999, where he studied with Fay Butler in Massachusetts. Butler is highly respected in the metalworking world because he is

James, an accomplished metalworker, shown welding in his shop.

one of only a handful of people who still know how to shape steel and other metals with early 20th-century tools, such as the Yoder power hammer and the English Wheel. These tools demand a high level of skill and can deliver finer results than mass-production techniques. Butler described James as "an extremely talented person with a great eye for design and style. He's one of the best welders I've ever come across."

CAREER HIGHLIGHTS

West Coast Choppers

James built several motorcycles in his little shop in Long Beach and sent pictures of them to biker magazines and design shops, hoping to get some attention. But for a few years, he was mostly ignored. The kind of motorcycles James liked building were very unfashionable when West Coast Choppers was starting out. Sedate, comfortable street bikes like the Harley-Davidson Fatboy were in style at that time. The rigid-frame, stripped-down choppers he created were considered a relic of the 1970s, favored only by outlaws and those out-of-touch with the times. James didn't care. As usual, he had his own vision and he stuck to it.

A West Coast Choppers bike is likely to include a lot of unusual features. For example, James likes to build bikes that have a foot clutch and a "jockey shifter," worked by hand—an old-fashioned setup that is difficult to handle but preferred by some chopper enthusiasts. He likes "ape hanger" handlebars, which require the rider to reach up and out, and long, stretched-out frames. He works the Maltese cross into his designs in many different ways, and many of his bikes have air filters fashioned to look like a spade from a deck of cards. On some of his choppers, he has adapted old cavalry swords for use as a functioning jockey shifter. One of his creations included special neon tubing for the spark plug wires, which glowed when powered up. Sections of metalwork that look like spiderwebs are frequently found on bikes from West Coast Choppers. Wild paint jobs, beautiful wheels, and clean, sweeping lines are also part of the West Coast Choppers aesthetic.

Jesse refuses to build bikes for people he doesn't like, and he spends long hours trying to figure out what makes a prospective owner tick. Then he tries to reflect that individual's special qualities in the design of their one-of-a-kind chopper. Once it is finished, James or one of his trusted assistants puts every motorcycle through hundreds of hours of riding under all conditions, making sure that there are no unexpected problems or bugs to be worked out. No formal warranty agreements are ever signed, but if anyone ever has a problem with their motorcycle, the West Coast Choppers crew will travel hundreds of miles to pick up the bike and bring it back to the shop in Long Beach to do whatever repairs might be needed.

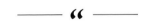

Respected metalworker Fay Butler described James as "an extremely talented person with a great eye for design and style. He's one of the best welders I've ever come across."

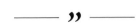

Celebrity Welder

Throughout the 1990s, James's reputation as a superb artist and craftsman slowly grew. The shop's location near Los Angeles, the heart of the entertainment industry, made it accessible for the many musicians and actors working there. The attention-getting looks and high-performance capabilities of West Coast Choppers had a lot of appeal for rock stars and high-profile actors and athletes. When such celebrities as Keanu Reeves, Kid Rock, and Shaquille O'Neal began buying choppers from James, the reputation of his shop quickly spread across the nation and, ultimately, the world. Soon there was a waiting list of the rich and famous who wanted to own a custom bike designed by Jesse James and built at West Coast Choppers. He expanded his shop and hired more employees, but even so, only about a dozen bikes are finished in a year. Each one takes about 400 to 1,000 hours of work and wil cost somewhere between $60,000 and $250,000.

One of James's customers was Thom Beers, a producer for the Discovery channel. He brought his motorcycle in for an overhaul at James's shop, and he was excited by the atmosphere there—the bright glare of the welding torches, the sound of engines being put through tests, metal being hammered, and over it all the blaring of the rap and acid rock music that's usually playing while the crews do their work. Beers decided the place was the perfect setting for a television special. With James's permission, Beers followed James and his workers for two weeks as they worked feverishly on several bikes they hoped to have ready in time for a rally at Daytona Beach, Florida.

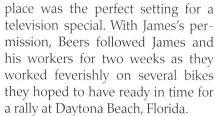

"Part of me really appreciates the attention," James said after the debut of his TV show, "but part of me thinks of all the metal guys, all the craftsmen who came before me, and all they did is work and punch a clock and no one gave them a TV show."

The finished show, called "Motorcycle Mania," aired in 2001, drawing the largest audience the Discovery channel had ever had. James's artistry and his no-nonsense persona translated well to the screen. Suddenly, the designer, builder, and self-proclaimed outlaw was as much a celebrity as many of his wealthy clients. James wasn't sure how he felt about his change in status. "Part of me really appreciates the attention," he said, "but part of me thinks of all the metal guys, all the craftsmen who came before me, and all they did is work and punch a clock and no one gave them a TV show." Despite his reservations, the show did so well that Discovery went on to produce "Motorcycle Mania II" in 2002 and "Motorcycle Mania III" in 2004. By that time, James had already started the show that would make him famous.

Boss of the "Monster Garage"

James's star status led the Discovery Channel to create "Monster Garage," a regular program built around the welder and his shop. "Monster Garage" first aired in 2002, and production continued until 2006. Each episode featured a different crew of five people with mechanical or metal-

In this scene from "Monster Garage," James is working on a project to transform a Mazda into a dune buggy.

working experience who had applied to be on the program. With Jesse as their boss, each team faced an assignment of transforming an ordinary vehicle into some sort of outrageous machine. They were given seven days to work on their project. The first was for designing, the next five days were for work, and the seventh day was set aside for testing the finished vehicle. The entire project could not cost more than $3,000 (later raised to $5,000). In theory, the end product was supposed to look like the original vehicle, but in practice, this rule wasn't always followed.

Some of the more memorable "Monster Garage" transformations included a PT Cruiser that could become a wood chipper, a school bus that could also function as a pontoon boat, a Mustang GT that became a high-speed lawnmower, a Volkswagen that could float, and a police car that doubled as a donut shop. One of James's particular favorites was a Ford ambulance that was modified so that it could do impressive wheelies. Part of the appeal of "Monster Garage" came from the vehicles themselves, but another element of its success was the way it showed the tensions and the cooperation between James and his crew members as they struggled to turn an idea into a reality, in time to meet the deadline.

Not all the monsters were successes. Some were ranked as failures because the crew couldn't meet the budget and deadline. Others didn't work properly when tested. Whatever the reason they were rejected, those projects deemed failures were destroyed in various ways devised by James. They were blown up, crushed, shot with handguns, smashed into walls, and torched with flamethrowers, among other things. The crazy concepts behind the monster vehicles and the spectacular ends they sometimes met made for winning entertainment. Episodes of "Monster Garage" were rebroadcast frequently and remained very popular on the Discovery channel. The show has been adapted as a video game, and models of the monster creations have been sold as toys.

James took the "Monster Garage" concept to Iraq with the special "Iraq Confidential with Jesse James," which aired in 2006. Besides taking a look at what conditions were like for military men and women in Iraq and visiting wounded soldiers in a hospital, James also worked with some of the troops to try transforming a bombed-out Humvee into a flying machine. The building project didn't work out as planned, but James found it a life-changing experience to enter a combat zone and see what soldiers go through on a daily basis. In yet another TV appearance, he was a contestant in the second season of "Celebrity Apprentice," a competition to see who would be selected for a demanding job. James remained in the running until the next to last episode of the second season in 2009.

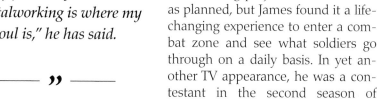

Although James has filled many roles, he identifies himself primarily as a welder. "Metalworking is where my soul is," he has said.

Taking Risks in "Jesse James Is a Dead Man"

James began a new television series in 2009 with "Jesse James Is a Dead Man." Over two million viewers tuned in to see the show's debut on the Spike channel. It featured James in a new, risk-taking situation each week. The idea wasn't to have him take foolish chances doing pointless stunts; instead, each episode showed him learning a new skill or trying out a new experience. He was set on fire while wearing a fireproof suit, took a flight in a military jet to experience zero gravity, and rode a motorcycle through arctic conditions. He raced in a World War II fighter plane and rode a rocket-powered motorcycle. He even broke the world record for a hydrogen-powered vehicle, hitting 199.7 miles per hour at the El Mirage Dry Lake in California on June 23, 2009. Despite the show's title, James survived the first season, but he did suffer a possible concussion and break two ribs and a bone in his elbow.

James in a scene from "Jesse James Is a Dead Man," a Spike TV series in which he tries a variety of new experiences, all involving risk-taking situations.

Life has become more complicated for James since he became a celebrity, but he has continued to design and build choppers in his shop. Although he fills many roles, he identifies himself primarily as a welder. "Metalworking is where my soul is," he has said. Unquestionably a master welder and creator of machines, he has also proven himself to be an astute businessman. Despite the high price tag on every West Coast Chopper, so much work goes into every custom bike that the profit margin is small. The company's financial success comes from many other sources. Most of its profits come from merchandise bearing the West Coast Chopper logo—hundreds of items, from sunglasses and keychains to bandanas and T-shirts. The company produces specialized lines of clothing for women, industrial workers, and children. There are West Coast Choppers aftermarket accessories for motorcycles, such as fenders and wheels, and the Choppers for Life line of kit bikes, for those who want some of the Jesse James magic but can't afford a custom-designed chopper.

HOME AND FAMILY

James married his first wife, Karla, around the early 1990s. They had two children, a daughter, Chandler, and a son, Jesse Jr. James and Karla divorced, and James married Janine Lindemulder. They had one daughter, Sunny, before divorcing in 2004. In 2006 James married actress Sandra Bullock, whom he met when she brought her godson to tour the West Coast Choppers shop.

HOBBIES AND OTHER INTERESTS

James has a collection of about 50 motorcycles and custom cars and trucks. He and his wife have several dogs, some of them adopted from shelters. They like taking in pets that might not otherwise find homes, due to disabilities or other problems. James also keeps pet sharks in a tank at the West Coast Choppers shop. He enjoys baking, with his specialty being almond tarts.

Because he believes strongly in improving industrial arts programs in schools, James established Jesse's Fund, a division of the Long Beach Education Foundation. This organization accepts donations of machinery and money for industrial-arts programs in the Long Beach area.

In addition to West Coast Choppers, James has started several other business ventures. In 2004, he began publishing *Garage,* a magazine about the custom car and motorcycle culture, and he also established his own TV production company, Payupsucker Productions. In addition, he owns a restaurant called Cisco Burger, named after one of his favorite dogs. Cisco Burger serves healthful food and makes use of solar power and other green technologies.

TELEVISION

"Motorcycle Mania I," 2001
"Motorcycle Mania II," 2002
"Motorcycle Mania III: Jesse James Rides Again," 2004
"Monster Garage," 2002-06
"Iraq Confidential with Jesse James," 2006
"Celebrity Apprentice," 2008-09 (contestant)
"Jesse James Is a Dead Man," 2009

HONORS AND AWARDS

Award for Contributions to Welding (American Welding Society): 2003

FURTHER READING

Books

Seate, Mike. *Jesse James: The Man and His Machines,* 2003

Periodicals

Autoweek, Aug. 18, 2003, p.16
Daily Variety, May 29, 2009, p.7
Los Angeles Times, May 24, 1009, p.D20
New York Times, Oct. 3, 2002, p.F1
People, Aug. 1, 2005, p.48; June 5, 2006, p.85; July 31, 2006, p.72
Popular Mechanics, Nov. 2007, p.90
USA Today, May 28, 2009, p.D7

ADDRESSES

Jesse James
The Discovery Channel
One Discovery Place
Silver Spring, MD 20910

Jesse James
West Coast Choppers
718 West Anaheim Street
Long Beach, CA 90813

WORLD WIDE WEB SITE

http://westcoastchoppers.com

Chuck Liddell 1969-

American Mixed Martial Arts Fighter
Former UFC Light Heavyweight World Champion,
known as "The Iceman"

BIRTH

Chuck Liddell was born in Santa Barbara, California, on December 17, 1969. His mother was Charlene Liddell Fisher, a single mom who worked for the county social services office but frequently took odd jobs to help support her family: Chuck, his older sister Laura, and his two younger brothers, Sean and Dan. Liddell's parents divorced when he was young and his father was not around while Chuck was growing up.

Instead, he found a male role model in his maternal grandfather and namesake, Charles Liddell. Chuck's grandparents helped their daughter raise their grandchildren after the high cost of living forced his mother to move the family in with her parents.

YOUTH

Liddell was a determined person even when he was very young. When he was a toddler, he began collapsing while walking and sometimes while standing; a doctor diagnosed faulty hip joints that couldn't keep his leg bones in their sockets. Although the doctor suggested braces as a treatment, they would have immobilized the toddler's legs, leaving him unable to walk for a time. Liddell's mother was afraid this would damage her young son's development and elected to give him physical therapy instead. For a year and a half she gave young Chuck two sessions of therapy almost every day. Although these sessions were very painful, by the time Liddell was three he could move around normally, except for a slight hitch in his gait.

Liddell enjoyed growing up with his grandma and "Pops" around. His grandfather taught him and his siblings to box when they were young, believing they should know how to defend themselves. His extended family also challenged the kids to learn, giving them regular vocabulary words and discussing politics around the dinner table. Liddell became a good student at school, involved in Boy Scouts and the chess club as well as athletics.

At the age of 12, Liddell discovered martial arts through the television show "Kung Fu Theatre." "They had demonstrations on every show and it got me really interested," he recalled. "I'd go to the library and look at all the books." His mother finally enrolled him at the dojo (a karate studio or school) of Jack Sabat, where Liddell studied the Koei-Kan style of karate. The school emphasized effective combat techniques, including striking methods and pressure points. Liddell loved learning and perfecting moves. "For me, it was never about getting the next level of belt," he said. "I just wanted to learn." He especially loved sparring and started out fighting with protective gear. He considered himself a "gym rat" and spent a lot of time analyzing which techniques were effective. At age 14, as a green belt, he came in second at a national

"For me, it was never about getting the next level of belt," Liddell said about taking karate classes. "I just wanted to learn."

karate competition. He loved competing and at his dojo he would fight anyone, no matter how much older or bigger they were. As he remembered, "the bigger and more painful the challenge, the more I wanted to do it."

EDUCATION

Liddell attended San Marcos High School in Santa Barbara, California, where he was a standout athlete and excellent student. He was a starter on the school's football team all four years; although he was "small and scrawny" until he filled out between the ages of 15 and 16, he didn't let anyone out-

Liddell while a wrestler at Cal Poly.

work him in practice or outplay him on the field. He played both center and linebacker on the football team, and in many games he was on the field for every play except for punts. His coach wanted him to take up another sport to keep in shape during the off-season, so Liddell chose wrestling. He was a natural at the sport, finishing third in a state tournament his junior year, mainly because of his superior conditioning. He also continued to study karate during high school. He was judged ready to test for black belt at 16, but he held off until he was an adult at his mother's request.

Liddell graduated from San Marcos High in 1988. He earned wrestling scholarships to several schools, but wanted to play football as well. When he was offered the chance to walk on the football team at California Polytechnic State University in San Luis Obispo, he decided to enroll there. He played football for a year, then decided to focus on wrestling so he wouldn't have to keep adjusting his weight for the different sports. He wrestled for four years and majored in accounting, eventually earning his Bachelor of Arts (BA) degree from Cal Poly in 1995. The university inducted him into their Athletics Hall of Fame in 2009.

CAREER HIGHLIGHTS

From Kickboxing to Mixed Martial Arts

As a graduation present to himself, Liddell got his scalp tattooed with the Japanese characters for Koei-Kan, which means "house of peace and prosperity" and is the name of the style of karate he practices. He got his scalp tattooed because he figured he could cover it with hair when he needed to apply for a regular job, but he didn't look for accounting work after graduation. He had worked as a bartender and bouncer during his college years and continued those jobs while he considered what he really wanted to do. He loved to fight and was good at it; he had gotten into fights on the street since high school, and he usually came away the winner. "I didn't start anything," he noted. "But I never made it too easy for a guy to back away." Still, he wasn't sure how he could make a living at fighting, besides teaching the occasional class at local dojos. After a college wrestling buddy went to Las Vegas to try professional kickboxing, Liddell eventually joined him at the gym of former champion Nick Blomgren.

Liddell began studying the Muay Thai style of fighting, which allows strikes from the elbows and knees, and started competing professionally. He made a steady living fighting on the weekends and bartending and teaching karate during the week. Then he met trainer John Hackleman, a former kickboxing champion who also had experience in judo and had created his own style of karate, which he called Hawaiian Kempo. Liddell began training at Hackelman's gym in San Luis Obispo, called The Pit, where he focused on conditioning as well as martial arts techniques. His workouts at the Pit taught Liddell that "being mentally tough is not a sometimes thing," he explained. "You don't turn it on and off. If you're not mentally tough in the gym while you are training, then when you're challenged in a fight, you will fold."

Liddell was having success as a professional kickboxer; he eventually ended up with an overall win-loss record of 20-2. This included championships from the United States Muay Thai Association and the World Kickboxing Association, as well as a U.S. title through the International Kickboxing Federation. Liddell was a good draw, bringing in a big audience to his fights, but he rarely earned more than $500 for a fight. His trainer Blomgren thought he should consider competing in the Ultimate Fighting Championship (UFC), a new mixed martial arts (MMA) league. It brought together fighters from different disciplines—including karate, judo, jiujitsu, and wrestling—to fight using both striking and grappling techniques. With its no-holds-barred style, the UFC was gaining fans through pay-per-view broadcasts. To prepare Liddell for MMA fighting, Blomgren sent him to train with John Lewis, a martial arts expert with particular expertise in Brazilian jiu-jitsu. Because of his wrestling experience, Liddell was hard to take down and keep down, but he needed more experience with the wide range of martial arts moves he might encounter in a mixed martial arts match. With Lewis's help, Liddell learned about administering and guarding against submission moves such as joint locks and improved his ability to fight while on the ground.

Starting with the UFC

Although Lewis had connections with the UFC, Liddell couldn't immediately break into the league. He competed in an MMA fight organized by Blomgren, knocking out his opponent with head kicks in the first round. Eventually he found a couple of managers who sent footage of that fight, as well as his kickboxing matches and training sessions, that helped secure him his first UFC fight. In 1998 Liddell debuted at UFC 17 as part of the undercard—an opening act, not the main draw—and was matched against fighter Noe Hernandez. The fight went the full 12 minutes with no knockouts, and the judges unanimously declared Liddell the winner. Just as important as the victory was the show Liddell put on: he fought aggressively, entertaining the crowd and making him someone to watch in the league.

Liddell couldn't get another UFC fight right away, however, as the league was having trouble finding state athletic organizations that would officially sanction their no-holds-barred style of fighting. In the meantime, the fighter headed to Brazil in August 1998, where he competed in the sixth International Vale Tudo Championship. Not only were the rules looser in Vale Tudo, a MMA-style competition with a long history in Brazil, but a fight going the distance would last a full 30 minutes. Liddell's opponent had won 13 of 15 fights, all by knockout, but the American held his ground and won another unanimous decision. He returned

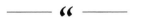

Working out at the gym taught Liddell that "being mentally tough is not a sometimes thing. You don't turn it on and off. If you're not mentally tough in the gym while you are training, then when you're challenged in a fight, you will fold."

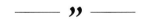

home to San Luis Obispo and in January 1999 opened SLO Kickboxing with Scott Adams, a college wrestling buddy. The gym became successful enough that Liddell was able to quit bartending jobs and focus solely on teaching and training in mixed martial arts.

Liddell returned to fight in UFC 19 against Jeremy Horn, and ended up losing when he encountered a choke hold he didn't know how to counter. But Liddell—who by now had earned the nickname "The Iceman" from his trainer because he never got nervous before a match—wasn't crushed by

*Liddell (left) and Tito Ortiz square off at the UFC 47 fight in 2004,
when Liddell knocked out Ortiz in the second round.*

his first MMA defeat. "I don't crawl into a shell after a loss," he revealed.
"What's the point? I knew I'd get another fight. I knew I'd get better. I knew
I'd find a way to win the next time." After the loss to Horn in early 1999,
Liddell racked up 10 consecutive MMA victories, seven of them in the UFC.
The league had turned a corner in 2001, when it was purchased by Liddell's
former manager, Dana White, and brothers Frank and Lorenzo Fertitta.
They introduced rules and regulations, standardized equipment, and established a scoring system and medical safeguards. The changes made the
sport more acceptable to state athletic commissions, and the UFC was soon
able to appear in more venues. They created a crowd-pleasing atmosphere
and got the fights returned to cable pay-per-view systems.

Becoming a Title Contender

By this time Liddell was considered a genuine title contender in the UFC
light heavyweight division. His upset technical knockout (TKO) of former

NCAA wrestling and UFC champ Kevin Randleman in 2001 gave him the qualifications to take on the then-current UFC champ, Tito Ortiz. It also allowed him to negotiate a new contract that guaranteed him between $25,000 and $45,000 per fight, with the chance to double the money if he won. While waiting for Ortiz to agree to a title shot, he knocked out contender Guy Mezger in a Pride tournament in Japan and earned a TKO against Renaldo Sobral in UFC 40. By mid-2003 Ortiz still hadn't granted him a title fight, so the UFC set up an "interim title" bout between Liddell and Randy Couture, a former UFC champ in both the heavyweight and light heavyweight divisions. Six weeks beforehand Liddell tore a ligament in his knee and had to change his training routine to avoid sharp lateral movements. In UFC 43 Liddell couldn't counter the experienced Couture's wrestling moves and lost by TKO in the third round.

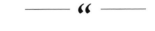

"Fighting is like chess, and boxing is like checkers," Liddell suggested. *"You have to defend against guys who are coming at you with all sorts of new tactics, new martial arts. You must be aware on different levels."*

There was only one way for Liddell to get back into title contention: keep fighting. He fought twice more in 2003 on the Pride circuit, winning by knockout against Alistair Overeem and losing by TKO to Quentin "Rampage" Jackson. He attributed the loss to poor training, and decided that in the future he would stick to training at The Pit. "I like being in one gym," he said. "I fight my way. I go to other gyms and train and learn from other places but when I'm training for a fight I train my way and train to fight the way I fight. If I lose I don't blame my camp." The loss to Jackson had one positive, however: it made Tito Ortiz, who had lost a title bout to Couture, finally agree to fight him. The fight, scheduled for UFC 47, would be one of the UFC's highest pay-per-view sellers to that date, and Liddell upped his training workouts in preparation. The work paid off, and Liddell knocked Ortiz out with a series of punches shortly after the start of the second round.

By the end of 2004, Liddell was not only one of the top light heavyweight contenders in the UFC, he was one of its most popular stars. UFC president Dana White was still trying to expand the league's audience, however, so he put together a reality show that would bring together 16 potential UFC fighters to battle for a professional contract. The contestants would be split into two teams, and Liddell agreed to coach one of them. Although Liddell and White believed that "The Ultimate Fighter" had great potential, they had difficulty convincing any networks to buy into the program. Finally Spike TV agreed to broadcast the show, although the UFC had to secure advertisers. When TUF debuted in January 2005, nearly 2 million viewers tuned in to the show, a huge number for a cable program. Not only did the show broaden the audience for the UFC, by showing the training that mixed martial arts fighting required, it demonstrated that the sport was more than brawling—it involved skill and strategy. "Fighting is like chess, and boxing is like checkers," Liddell suggested. "You have to defend against guys who are coming at you with all sorts of new tactics, new martial arts. You must be aware on different levels." When the final episode of the series aired, it brought Spike TV its highest ratings ever, over three million viewers.

Claiming the UFC Title

A week after "The Ultimate Fighter" finale scored with audiences, Liddell got another shot at the UFC light heavyweight title in a rematch against Randy Couture. The Iceman trained hard for the match, focusing on strength and stamina and studying their previous bout to come up with a better strategy. At UFC 52 on April 16, 2005, Liddell finally claimed the UFC title by knocking out Couture two minutes into the first round. Over the next two years he successfully defended the title four times, each time by TKO. These victories included one over Jeremy Horn—one of the only three men who had ever beaten him, and a fighter who had never before lost by knockout—as well as rematches against Couture, Sobral, and Ortiz.

The wins were a product of hard work. Liddell's typical training schedule involved workouts three times a day, five times a week, with one extra day off per month to let off steam and party. "If I'm feeling burned out, I go out and get loose and have a good time," he related. "Then I take the day off Sunday and come back on Monday ready to train."

Liddell finally lost his UFC title in 2007, in a rematch against Quinton "Rampage" Jackson in UFC 71. He attributed the loss to a mistake in technique, not a loss of confidence. "Like both of the other guys I went back and avenged, I think I should have beaten him the first time," Liddell explained. "Afterward, I thought I messed up. I should go out there and be able to beat him." He lost his next match as well, in a split decision against Keith Jardine in UFC 76, before winning a unanimous decision against former Pride league champ Wanderlei Silva in UFC 79. He then lost his next two matches, in UFC 88 to Rashad Evans and in UFC 97 to Mauricio Rua, both by knockout. About the 2008 loss to Evans, he noted: "I got a little impatient. I got in a bad position and got caught. I don't think it's because

Liddell (left) fights Keith Jardine at UFC 76 in 2007.

I'm predictable. You know I'm going to come and try to knock you out. But I don't think it's that simple." He planned to change up his strategies and techniques for future matches, a challenge he found interesting: "Discovery is still a draw for me, in the same way it made me want to keep going in karate when I was a teenager," he said. "Fighting is as much about the internal challenge as it is the external battle."

The Face of the Sport

After winning the UFC title in 2004, Liddell's public recognition and celebrity continued to increase. Even after losing the title in 2007, he was still the most recognizable figure in the league, the face of the UFC. He began making appearances as himself in films and on television. He had an extended role in 2007 on an episode of the television series "Entourage," and voiced his own character on "The Simpsons" in 2009. He also tried minor acting roles: in the 2006 television pilot of "Blade: The Series," he made an appearance as a tattoo artist, and in the 2007 film *The Death and Life of Bobby Z*, he played a tough prison inmate named Mad Dog.

Liddell's biggest challenge, however, was appearing on the reality show "Dancing with the Stars" on ABC, taking advantage of a long break between fights. He planned to "go out and be myself and show what kind of people we do have in this sport," he remarked. "I'm sure the reaction will be mixed. My friends are [going to] be excited and I'll never hear the end of it because they'll make fun of me, but it should be fun and I think everyone will like it." Liddell and his dancing partner Anna Trebunskaya lasted four episodes before being voted off the show.

Liddell has spent much of his time traveling and promoting the UFC, but he continues to find celebrity a difficult adjustment. "Even after all this time, I still don't know how to take it," he remarked. "I almost feel like saying, 'sorry.' I love the fact that people appreciate the sport and how tough it is, but it's still strange to be a celebrity." He is known for taking time with his fans, however, especially kids and those in the military and emergency services. "Those fans were there for me when I started, I got involved with them. I appreciate it.... I get to do what I love for a living. If taking a few minutes out of my time is part of the price, great. I try to remember, even when it gets hard, I remember this is the first time this guy gets to meet me. He's excited. I try to give enthusiasm back."

> "All I've been doing my whole life is training to compete. It's a hard thing to give up for an athlete. It's hard to stop competing after so many years," Liddell observed. "I'm going to fight as long as my body's working.... I enjoy it that much."

In 2009, as he was inducted into the UFC Hall of Fame, Liddell still had enthusiasm for fighting and wasn't ready to retire. "All I've been doing my whole life is training to compete," he observed. "It's a hard thing to give up for an athlete. It's hard to stop competing after so many years." He hoped to continue fighting for the foreseeable future. "I'm going to fight as long as my body's working," he noted. "I keep saying another two to four years. And I hope in two years I can say it's still two to four years. I enjoy it that much." In 2009, it was announced that Liddell would face off against Tito Ortiz one more time: first as opposing coaches on season 11 of "The Ultimate Fighter," and then once again in the UFC Octagon. For the future, Liddell has suggested that he might become a trainer. "I like the personal interaction. I like working on the finer points, improving the little things that can make a big difference that the younger fighters don't always know about." Whenever he decides to officially retire from fighting, he will likely stay with the UFC in some capacity. "I don't think you could get me away from it," he noted. "I love this sport."

Liddell with dancing partner Anna Trebunskaya on "Dancing with the Stars."

HOME AND FAMILY

Although Liddell has never married, he is the proud father of two children, both born to former girlfriends. Daughter Trista was born in September 1997 to Casey Noland, while son Cade was born in October 1998 to Lori Geyer. Liddell loves spending time with his kids, and has been known to fly in for a single day just to visit. He still lives in San Luis Obispo, where he has a comfortable home that has been profiled on MTV's "Cribs."

HOBBIES AND OTHER INTERESTS

Liddell enjoys the perks of the celebrity lifestyle, particularly the nightlife. He likes to go out to dance or sing karaoke, usually with a group of buddies that has been with him since college. He likes driving fast cars, especially the Ferrari F430 Spider that UFC President White gave to him as a bonus. He is also known for his love of pedicures and likes to paint his toenails, especially in black or even pink.

Liddell makes frequent appearances for various charities. He signed a prototype toy of himself to be auctioned for Special Olympics and was the first mixed martial artist to participate in the charity golf tournament that supports the Lance Armstrong Foundation. The Iceman has also attended Celebrity Fight Night, which helps support the Muhammad Ali Parkinson Center and other charities, and has worked with groups that assist low-income and at-risk youth through martial arts. He is also known to take time to visit young fans with special needs and military veterans.

HONORS AND AWARDS

North American Heavyweight Champion (United States Muay Thai Association): approx. 1996-97

Amateur International Rules U.S. Super Heavyweight Champion (International Kickboxing Federation): 1996-97

World Light Heavyweight Champion (Ultimate Fighting Championship): 2004-07

Guys Choice Award (Spike TV): 2007, for Most Dangerous Man

Hall of Fame (Ultimate Fighting Championship): 2009

FURTHER READING

Books

Liddell, Chuck, with Chad Millman. *Iceman: My Fighting Life,* 2008

Periodicals

Atlanta Journal-Constitution, Sep. 6, 2008, p.D1

ESPN The Magazine, May 21, 2007
Fight! Magazine, Sep. 2008, p.40
Las Vegas Review-Journal, Aug. 18, 2009
Men's Fitness, Apr. 2007, p.94
Miami Herald, May 24, 2007
MMA United, June 2009, p.28
TapouT Magazine, issue 26, 2008, p.41
USA Today, Sep. 8, 2008, p. C2; Apr. 17, 2009, p.C10

Online Articles

http://www.mmafighting.com
(MMA Fighting, "Chuck Liddell: 'Hard for an Athlete to Quit What He's Done His Whole Life,'" Aug. 13, 2009)

ADDRESS

Chuck Liddell
Zinkin Entertainment
5 River Park Place West, Suite 203
Fresno, CA 93720

WORLD WIDE WEB SITE

http://www.icemanmma.com

MARY MARY
Erica Campbell 1974?-
Tina Campbell 1975?-

American Gospel Singers
Grammy Award-Winning Creators of the Hit
Albums *Thankful* and *The Sound*

EARLY YEARS

Mary Mary is the gospel singing duo of sisters Erica Campbell and Tina Campbell. Although their exact birth dates are not publicized, most sources indicate that Erica Monique Atkins was born in 1974, and Trecina "Tina" Evette Atkins was born

65

in 1975. Later, they both married men with the last name Campbell, though their husbands are not related to each other. Their father, Eddie Atkins, was a postal worker, youth minister, and church choir director before he became a Pentecostal pastor. Their mother, Thomasina Atkins, was a homemaker and church piano player. Erica and Tina have five sisters and one brother.

Erica and Tina grew up in Inglewood, California, a suburb of Los Angeles. Their family was poor and sometimes struggled financially. "We lived on faith," Tina recalled. "Looking back, it's hard to see how we didn't become homeless. Each year our parents were $7,000 short of what was needed and just had to trust God. We ate noodles every day, so we never went hungry. We didn't know we were poor because we had so much love and faith. We had a lot of fun, too. The church was our recreational center." One Christmas was particularly memorable, according to Tina: "Since it's the thought that counts, we gave one another thoughts for Christmas." Erica explained, "What we did is take a piece of paper, and we all wrote down individually what we thought of each sister and the cousins and my mom and dad. Some were funny, and some of them were touching. But we had so much fun, and I don't think we will ever forget that."

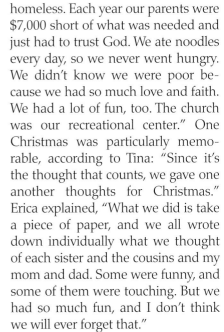

> *"We lived on faith," Tina recalled. "Looking back, it's hard to see how we didn't become homeless. Each year our parents were $7,000 short of what was needed and just had to trust God. We ate noodles every day, so we never went hungry. We didn't know we were poor because we had so much love and faith. We had a lot of fun, too. The church was our recreational center."*

Their parents were strict and kept a close watch over their children's activities. The family was very involved in the church community and attended the Evangelistic Church of God in Christ. As the children of a church choir director and later pastor, the Erica and Tina spent a lot of time at church, basically seven days a week, and gospel music was a constant presence in their life. The Atkins children first sang in their church choir and later went along with their father to sing during his ministry visits to what Erica called "seemingly godforsaken parts of the inner city." The Atkins children were forbidden to listen to any non-gospel music at home, although Erica and Tina were exposed to other kinds of music, including hip-hop and R&B, while at school and in their neighborhood. "We were born and raised in urban communities," Tina explained. "And so what happened in the community was that the sound of the community, the look, the lingo, all of those things—we were exposed to that."

CAREER HIGHLIGHTS

Erica and Tina began their singing careers working separately. They each performed as backup singers with such R&B artists as Brian McKnight, Brandy, Eric Benet, and Kenny Lattimore. Touring with these performers gave them each a chance to develop their talents as well as their independence. In 1995, Erica and Tina both went on tour with the traveling gospel music show *Mama I'm Sorry*. Later, they toured together again with the gospel show *Sneaky*. With these productions, the sisters performed up to eight shows each week.

During these years, Erica and Tina learned a lot about the business side of the music industry. They were able to observe all of the off-stage activities and responsibilities held by performers, including media appearances, interviews, and working with producers and agents. This experience helped Erica and Tina to gain a better understanding of the business. Tina said of these early years, "I won't say that it was our ministry to go sing background with different R&B artists that were singing, you know, about different things [that are] not necessarily Christian, but I do think that that was part of God's plan for us."

Erica and Tina formed the group Mary Mary in 1996. The name Mary Mary is taken from the two women named Mary in the Bible. "It's inspired by the two Marys: Christ's mother, who many people think of as perfect, and Mary Magdalene, who, well, isn't," Tina clarified. "But meeting Jesus caused Mary Magdalene to change her life and become one of his strongest followers. So we tell people it doesn't matter who you are or where you're from, we all can be changed by God's love."

Mary Mary first got a music contract as songwriters. They created songs that were recorded by other performers, including gospel star Yolanda Adams and gospel group 702. Their first big break came in 1998, when their original song "Let Go, Let God" was included on the *Prince of Egypt* movie soundtrack. Their song "Dance" was included on the soundtrack for the movie *Dr. Doolittle* in that same year. Then their next big success came when Yolanda Adams recorded two of their songs, and the album went platinum. These successes lead to a recording contract for Mary Mary in 1999, and Erica and Tina began to work on songs for their own record release.

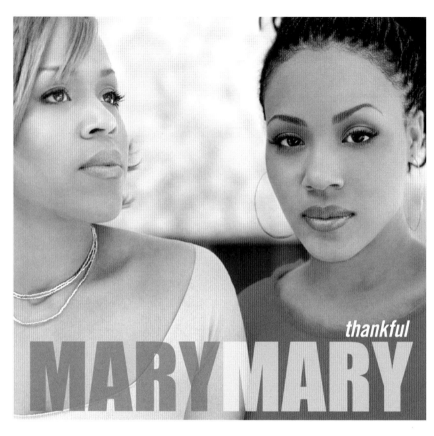

Mary Mary's debut album, Thankful, *was enjoyed by both Christian and mainstream audiences.*

Thankful

Mary Mary's debut album, *Thankful,* was released in 2000. *Thankful* included mostly original songs written by Erica and Tina, along with versions of the gospel classics "What a Friend We Have in Jesus" and "Wade in the Water." The record blended gospel, R&B, hip-hop, and dance rhythms in a surprising combination that appealed to both Christian and mainstream audiences. Erica described their approach to creating the record, saying, "We wanted to do something different, kind of innovative. We wanted to give the world the gospel according to Mary Mary, which is different from how others have done."

The breakout first single "Shackles (Praise You)" featured a dance beat that propelled it to the top of the Billboard music charts. The song became a Top 10 hit in the U.S., United Kingdom, France, the Netherlands, and Australia.

The video for "Shackles (Praise You)" went into heavy rotation on MTV. A music critic for *People* magazine praised Mary Mary for their "funky hip-hop beats and lush harmonies worthy of Destiny's Child." *Ebony* magazine said that Mary Mary's "voices are [steeped] in soulful intensity, and the songs they sing thump with a thunderous bass that makes you want to let loose and dance." *Thankful* won a Grammy Award for Best Contemporary Gospel Album.

Incredible

Mary Mary's second record, *Incredible,* was released in 2002. With *Incredible,* Mary Mary once again used R&B and hip-hop beats to draw a younger generation of listeners to gospel music. "Gospel tells you about what God can do, it tells you the good news of Jesus," Erica remarked. "Because our music is so hip-hop and has an urban feel, a lot of people think, 'Oh, it's inspirational, it's contemporary.' It can be. But listen to what we're saying in our songs which tell the message of Christ specifically."

"Gospel tells you about what God can do, it tells you the good news of Jesus," Erica remarked. "Because our music is so hip-hop and has an urban feel, a lot of people think, 'Oh, it's inspiriational, it's contemporary.' It can be. But listen to what we're saying in our songs which tell the message of Christ specifically."

Incredible was a huge hit for Mary Mary, capturing the No. 1 spot on Billboard's Top Christian Album and Top Gospel Album charts at the same time. The record was both a commercial and critical success, earning praise from critics. *Essence* magazine congratulated Mary Mary for their ability to "combine traditional gospel concepts with hip-hop rhythms and R&B balladry to deliver straightforward messages of God's love through every soul-stirring song." A music critic for the *Baltimore Sun* noted that *Incredible* "sounds like an R&B album that just happens to mention Jesus a lot."

After the release of *Incredible,* Mary Mary took a three-year break from recording new music. During this time, Erica and Tina wrote their autobiography, *Transparent,* which was published in 2002. They also appeared in the 2003 musical comedy *The Fighting Temptations.*

Mary Mary and A Mary Mary Christmas

The duo's self-titled third record *Mary Mary* was released in 2005 and debuted in the No. 1 position on the Billboard Gospel Album sales chart.

Mary Mary produced the hit single "Heaven" and once again drew critical acclaim. *People* magazine praised *Mary Mary* for its "decidedly contemporary style that blurs the lines between sacred and secular music." *Ebony* called the record "jubilant" with "enhanced emotional depth, earthy soul, and stronger faith." *Mary Mary* won an American Music Award for Favorite Inspirational/Christian Contemporary Artist, and was nominated for a Grammy Award as Best Contemporary Soul Gospel Album.

Mary Mary's fourth record, *A Mary Mary Christmas*, was released in 2006. This collection includes versions of holiday standards, hymns, and original new Christmas songs written by Mary Mary. As Tina observed, "The CD captures the holiday spirit and the true reason for Christmas. The spirit of it all. All the elements of the season." *A Mary Mary Christmas* was generally well received and praised for its introduction of new contemporary Christmas songs.

The Sound

In 2008, Mary Mary released *The Sound*, their fifth record. *The Sound* became an instant success, reaching No. 1 on Billboard's Gospel chart. It was also Mary Mary's first big crossover hit, rising to the No. 2 spot on Billboard's R&B/Hip-Hop chart. The popularity of *The Sound* with R&B and hip-hop audiences as well as gospel music lovers proved that Mary Mary had a growing fan base. A music reviewer for SoulTracks.com noted that this release was surprising because "Mary Mary can sound so new—and maybe even better—five records into their career." Tina explained, "We try to make sure everything we put out there represents what we represent, that is true to us first—lyrically, creatively, sonically. We want it to be banging, on point. We want it to be respected across the board."

The Sound earned Mary Mary many awards in 2009: they won an NAACP Image Award and a BET Award, both for Best Gospel Artist, and the song "Get Up" won a Grammy Award for Best Gospel Performance and a Dove Award for Urban Recorded Song of the Year. "That song embodies what the whole album is about, Erica revealed. "It asks people 'Why are you waiting? Why do you care what other people think?' It reminds us that your beginning can be whatever you want it to be."

But not everyone was pleased with Mary Mary's performance on *The Sound*. The song "God in Me" caused some controversy among gospel music fans because of its secular subject matter. The lyrics refer to owning flashy cars and designer clothes, unusual topics for a gospel song. And at first, Mary Mary wasn't even sure they wanted to record "God in Me,"

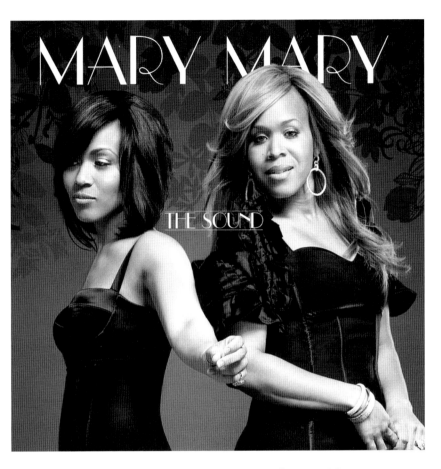

The Sound *was a big crossover success for Mary Mary,*
reaching No. 2 on the Billboard R&B/Hip Hop chart.

Erica recalled. "But when I started paying attention to what it was saying
… this is how, this is why, this is what has enabled me, I was like, 'You got
me!'" Erica said. Ultimately, the song won a lot of admirers: Mary Mary
won the 2010 Grammy Award for Best Gospel Song, a songwriting award,
for "God in Me."

Despite this controversy, *The Sound* has ultimately been received as an up-
lifting, empowering, and inspirational contribution to contemporary
gospel music. SoulTracks.com called *The Sound* a "treat from beginning to
end and a great reminder that effective praise comes in all forms—and
maybe is even more effective when it simply sounds this good." Tina explained, "The album is about overcoming and thriving. I think this record

71

is kind of a perfect soundtrack for where America is right now, for what we're going through with the economy and other challenges. We need strong faith in our sovereign God."

Responding to Criticism

Mary Mary's success has drawn some additional criticism over the years. Some people in the gospel music community feel that their music is not true gospel because of their use of secular musical styles. The sisters generally take this criticism in stride and remain confident in their talents. "It's all good; you just have to brush that dirt off your shoulder," Tina remarked. "When we go into the studio we are very true to ourselves. Yes, we are aware of the trends, but we don't force things or try to become something else. We write from our hearts and sing about what we believe in and stay true to who we are."

"Sometimes people think we're a little bit sexy. I don't have a problem with that," Tina said. "Some people in church unfortunately are not aware that we are not supposed to just be there. We're supposed to go out and reach people. And you can't go out with a long white dress on and think they're going to pay attention to you."

Erica and Tina have also been criticized for appearing on stage and in photos wearing form-fitting clothing. "Sometimes people think we're a little bit sexy. I don't have a problem with that," Tina said. "Some people in church unfortunately are not aware that we are not supposed to just be there. We're supposed to go out and reach people. And you can't go out with a long white dress on and think they're going to pay attention to you."

In fact, Erica and Tina use their music to talk about God and Christianity. "We want to encourage people to expect big things of God," Erica stressed. "A lot of people just want a healthy family or to pay their bills, and don't really expect great things from God. We don't want to live just-average Christian lives because we don't serve an average God. He's extraordinary. Of course, we can't just sit back and expect great things; we need to do great things." Tina added, "We represent a great, big God who is excellent, so we like to think that our work represents that, too. God's blessings are new every day. He's blowing our minds every day. We should be able to speak to a new day in a new way."

Erica Campbell (left) and Tina Campbell (right) at the 2009 Grammy Awards, after winning Best Gospel Performance for "Get Up."

Mary Mary has helped to create an updated sound and image for gospel music with their unique combination of traditional gospel themes and elements of R&B, urban, hip-hop, electronica, and dance music. This mix of diverse musical styles has helped Mary Mary bring gospel music to a new audience. "There's always someone who has music that will reach an unchurched audience," Erica commented. "That's definitely the position Mary Mary holds. Growing up, we didn't look at people who didn't go to church any differently from those who did. When it comes to our music, our music is for everyone. Everyone needs to know that God loves them."

Future Plans

Mary Mary has many plans for the future, both in and out of the recording studio. "We don't want to limit ourselves to just singing. All the gifts and all the talents and all the great entrepreneurial ideas that God has given us, we want to use them," Tina said. "I don't care if you're making a statement in fashion, doing movies that reflect who you are, whatever it is that you decide to do outside of just one thing—if God has gifted you, you should do it all to bring Him glory."

Mary Mary has released a bath and beauty line called Be U and plans to develop a clothing line and a series of books, music, and interactive computer games for children. Erica and Tina are also executive producers and featured judges on the BET cable network series "Sunday Best," an "American Idol"-style competition for gospel singers. "We consider ourselves to be unpredictable," Tina said. "We like to think that we're innovative and original so you cannot figure out what our next move is and you can't really define our ability or what you think the expectations are."

MARRIAGE AND FAMILY

In 2000, Tina married Teddy Campbell, a musician and drummer in the "American Idol" band. They have three daughters, Cierra, Laiah, Meela, and one son, TJ. Erica married Warryn Campbell, who is Mary Mary's music producer, in 2001. They have one daughter, Krista. Teddy Campbell and Warryn Campbell share a last name, but they are not related.

Balancing their careers and families is the highest priority for both Erica and Tina. "We try not to be gone more than four or five days at a time," Tina said. "We've got to be there to put our kids to bed, pray with them, and go over homework with them. Parenting is hands-on, and you can't do that through the phone or text messages." Erica added, "If Tina and I are going to be gone for more than four or five days, we bring our families with us. If I'm a public success and a private failure at home, then I've failed. We have to make sure we succeed at home and the only way to do that is love." Erica explained that the support of their families is critical to Mary Mary's success. "Real success starts with all the love you have in your heart. It's about family and having the emotional support of those you love." Tina added, "It can inspire you and catapult you in so many amazing ways. All the money in the world can't help you do that."

RECORDINGS

Thankful, 2000
Incredible, 2002
Mary Mary, 2005
A Mary Mary Christmas, 2006
The Sound, 2008

HONORS AND AWARDS

Dove Award (Gospel Music Channel): 2001, Urban Album of the Year, for *Thankful* and Urban Recorded Song of the Year, for "Shackles (Praise You)"; 2002, Urban Recorded Song of the Year, for "Thank You"; 2003, Contemporary Gospel Recorded Song of the Year, for "In the Morning"; 2004, Urban Recorded Song of the Year, for "Dance, Dance, Dance"; 2006, Contemporary Gospel Album of the Year, for *Mary Mary*; 2009, Urban Recorded Song of the Year, for "Get Up"

Grammy Award (Recording Academy): 2001, Best Contemporary Soul Gospel Album, for *Thankful*; 2009, Best Gospel Performance, for "Get Up"; 2010, Best Gospel Song, for "God in Me" (with Warryn Campbell)

Soul Train Music Award: 2001, Best Gospel Album, for *Thankful*

Stellar Awards (Gospel Music Channel): 2001, Group/Duo of the Year, Contemporary Group/Duo of the Year, New Artist of the Year and Contemporary CD of the Year, for *Thankful*

American Music Award: 2005, Favorite Contemporary Inspirational Music Artist; 2009, Favorite Contemporary Inspirational Music Artist

BET Award: 2009, Best Gospel Artist

NAACP Image Award: 2009, Best Gospel Artist

FURTHER READING

Periodicals

Ebony, Sep. 2000, p.100; Dec. 2006, p.50; Jan. 2007, p.86
Essence, Feb. 2004, p.120; Nov. 2008, p.68; Nov. 2009, p.20
Jet, Sep. 23, 2002, p.19; May 11, 2009, p.36
Today's Christian Woman, Mar.-Apr. 2009, p.22

Online Articles

http://www.mtv.com/music/artist/mary_mary/artist.jhtml
    (MTV, "Mary Mary," undated)
http://www.npr.org/templates/story/story.php?storyId=102868367
    (NPR Music, "Mary Mary: Pop-Gospel Disciples," Apr. 10, 2009)

http://www.soultracks.com/mary_mary.htm
  (Soul Tracks, "Mary Mary," undated)
http://www.vh1.com/artists/az/mary_mary/artist.jhtml
  (VH1, "Mary Mary," undated)
http://new.music.yahoo.com/mary-mary
  (Yahoo Music, "Mary Mary," undated)

ADDRESS

Mary Mary
Columbia Records
550 Madison Avenue
New York, NY 10022

WORLD WIDE WEB SITE

http://www.mary-mary.com

Stephenie Meyer 1973-

American Author
Creator of the Bestselling Novel Series, "The Twilight Saga"

BIRTH

Stephenie Meyer was born Stephenie Morgan on December 24, 1973, in Hartford, Connecticut. She was the second of six children born to Stephen and Candy Morgan; her siblings are Emily, Heidi, Paul, Seth, and Jacob. The unusual form of her first name is the result of her father's decision to add "ie" to the end of his name rather than using the conventional spelling, "Stephanie."

YOUTH

When Meyer was four years old, her family moved to Phoenix, Arizona, where her father began working as the chief financial officer at a contracting company. Growing up in a large family was good for her as a writer, she has said. It helped her understand many different personality types and the way people interact. "My siblings sometimes crop up as characters in my stories," she commented. Her father enjoyed reading to his children—not from books written for kids, but from whatever he was interested in at the time. Because of her father's influence, Meyer never really read much children's literature, even when she was young. Instead, her favorites included classics like *Jane Eyre* by Charlotte Bronte and *Pride and Prejudice* by Jane Austen.

EDUCATION

Meyer attended Chaparral High School in Scottsdale, Arizona. It was an affluent school, "the kind of place where every fall a few girls would come back to school with new noses," she commented, "and there were Porsches in the student lot." She graduated from high school in 1992. Meyer won a National Merit Scholarship and selected Brigham Young University in Provo, Utah. Meyer was raised as a member of the Church of Jesus Christ of Latter-Day Saints (commonly known as the Mormon church), and BYU is run by the Mormon church. The atmosphere there is quiet and conservative, which was fine with her. "On the list of the biggest party schools in the country," she remarked, "BYU consistently and proudly finishes dead last." In 1997, she graduated with a Bachelor of Arts (BA) degree in English.

CAREER HIGHLIGHTS

Even though she was an avid reader and had studied literature in college, Meyer never had any ambition of making her living as a writer. She considered going to law school, but her plans changed after she became involved with Christiaan "Pancho" Meyer. The two had known each other casually since childhood, and they attended the same church. It wasn't until the summer before her senior year of college, however, that they got to know each other well. The relationship took off, and they married the year she graduated from college. After that, she worked as a receptionist briefly, and even made a couple of starts at writing some stories. She gave up working outside the home, however, when she became pregnant with her first child, Gabe. Two more sons, Seth and Eli, soon followed. Any interest Meyer had in writing was sidetracked by the demands of taking care of three small boys.

Meyer was glad to stay at home with her children, but their early years were a challenging time. Her sons were fussy babies, sleeping very little and crying a lot. Up with them at all hours of the night, Meyer became sleep-deprived herself. At times she felt she was merely going through the motions, walking through life like a zombie. On June 2, 2003, however, a dramatic transformation began in her life. On that morning, she had a very vivid dream. It concerned two teenagers conversing in a beautiful meadow, brightly lit by sunlight but situated deep within a forest. Despite the beauty of the scene, there was a sense of danger in the air. The boy and the girl were having an intense discussion about the problems they faced because the girl was human and the boy was a vampire, and they were in love.

> *Meyer attended Brigham Young University, where the atmosphere is quiet and conservative. That was fine with her. "On the list of the biggest party schools in the country," she remarked, "BYU consistently and proudly finishes dead last."*

From Dream to Multi-Book Contract

This dream was so powerful and so interesting that Meyer didn't want to get out of bed after she woke up. She knew she had many things to do that day, but she lay there for a while, savoring every detail of the dream. She continued to think of it after she got up and began her daily routine. As soon as she could find a spare moment, she wrote down everything at she could remember. The pages she wrote that day eventually became Chapter 13 of the book *Twilight.*

From that day onward, Meyer's life changed. The characters she had dreamed continued to dominate her thoughts. As she went about her business, running errands, changing diapers, taking children to swim lessons and other activities, she was thinking about the boy and the girl, hearing them converse in her mind. Whenever an opportunity presented itself, she hurried to the computer to type out all she had been thinking, fleshing out the story that had started with her dream and grown from there. First of all, she continued from the scene in the forest clearing and wrote until she reached the end of the story. Then, she backed up and started at the beginning, writing up to Chapter 13. She kept a notebook by her bedside so she could write down any ideas that struck in the middle of the night.

Meyer started writing Twilight
after being inspired by a dream about Bella and Edward.

Meyer was a little alarmed by her obsession, especially because she'd never had the slightest interest in vampires before that summer. Despite a wide range of reading interests, horror was the one genre that she had never enjoyed. At first, she was too embarrassed even to tell her husband what was going on, and he wondered why she rarely seemed to sleep or let him use the family computer. For a while, only her older sister Emily knew about the story. She urged Meyer to continue working on it. Once Meyer let her husband in on her secret, he also encouraged her to keep writing.

Meyer wanted to set her story somewhere with abundant rainfall. Her research showed her that the rainiest place in the United States is the Olympic Peninsula, in the state of Washington. Looking at more detailed maps, she noticed the small town of Forks, surrounded by forest and situated close to the La Push Reservation of the Quileute Tribe of Native Americans. The Quileute mythology gave Meyer still more inspiration for her story. She decided to use Forks as her setting, not even changing the name of the town. In fact, "Forks" was her original title for the book, one she says she still likes.

> **"**
>
> *"It certainly wasn't belief in my fabulous talent that made me push forward," Meyer said about trying to get her first book published. "I think it was just that I loved my characters so much, and they were so real to me, that I wanted other people to know them, too."*
>
> **"**

By August 2003, Meyer had finished her story—130,000 words of it, written just for fun. After reading the whole thing, however, her sister Emily urged her to look into having it published. Meyer didn't know anything about the book business, and once she started investigating, she felt quite intimidated. "It certainly wasn't belief in my fabulous talent that made me push forward," she said. "I think it was just that I loved my characters so much, and they were so real to me, that I wanted other people to know them, too."

Meyer sent about 15 queries to publishing houses and authors' agents she had located by searching the Internet. Some didn't answer at all, several sent rejection letters, but one—an assistant at the Writers House literary agency—responded enthusiastically. Soon Meyer got a phone call from Jodi Reamer, an agent at Writers House. Reamer saw the great potential in Meyer's work and wanted to represent her. The two of them worked together to polish the manuscript for a couple of weeks. At Reamer's suggestion, they gave it a new, more marketable title: *Twilight.* On the Wednesday before Thanksgiving, Reamer sent the manuscript to editors at several publishing houses.

The following Monday, Reamer called Meyer to say that an editor at the Little, Brown publishing house had made an offer of $300,000 for *Twilight.* Meyer could hardly believe this incredible news, but she was even more shocked when Reamer said she'd turned down the offer, holding out for more money. It seemed crazy to Meyer, but Reamer knew what she was doing. In the end, eight publishers bid against each other for the rights to *Twilight,* and Meyer ended up with a $750,000, three-book contract from Little, Brown, as well as selling the film rights to her first book. Her road from dream to six-figure, multi-book deal had unfolded within a matter of six months, an almost unbelievable success story.

Twilight, a Vampire Romance

Twilight proved to be every bit as popular as Meyer's agent or publisher could have hoped. There was a lot of excitement and publicity about the book even before it reached the public. Within five weeks of its release in October 2005, *Twilight* was on the *New York Times* bestseller list. Entering at the No. 5 position, it soon reached the top and stayed there for many weeks. Sales remained strong years after its initial publication, spurred by the popularity of sequels and the movie adaptations.

Twilight is narrated by Bella Swan, a 17-year-old girl. As the story begins, she is leaving Phoenix, where she has lived with her mother, to move to the town of Forks, Washington, where her father is the police chief. On the first day in her new school, she notices a strange, pale, beautiful boy staring intently at her. He is Edward Cullen, and what Bella doesn't realize is that he is a vampire who appears as the 17-year-old he was when he became immortal, about 100 years earlier.

Edward is intensely attracted to Bella. With the wisdom gained over 100 years of life, he recognizes her as his great love. In addition to his feelings of pure love, however, he also has a ravenous desire to taste her blood. He resists this, as he resists all such temptations. Edward and his family are part of a coven of vampires that choose not to take human life. Instead, they have disciplined themselves to feed only on the blood of animals, hunting at night, as they never need to sleep. There are other covens, however, that make no attempt to resist their thirst for human blood. Tension in the story comes both from the dangerous nature of Edward's love for Bella and from the threat of vampire covens that prey on humans. A re-

The movie Twilight *proved to be as popular as the book—if not more so.*

viewer for *Publishers Weekly* called *Twilight* a "riveting first novel, propelled by suspense and romance in equal parts."

Meyer has insisted that she writes stories, not messages. When asked about the main theme running through *Twilight,* however, she noted that one important idea is that we all have free will. That concept is demonstrated by the Cullens' decision not to take human life, even though they are vampires. "It doesn't matter where you're stuck in life or what you think you have to do; you can always choose something else. There's always a different path," she said.

With her story, Meyer touched on feelings that many teenagers could understand—of being different, feeling like an outcast, and trying to control powerful impulses. She also offered a unique depiction of vampires. The author had never read any of the classic or contemporary works of vampire literature, such as Bram Stoker's *Dracula* or the novels of Anne Rice. Her characters don't share the traits often associated with vampires. In addition to being able to choose not to drink human blood, they are able to venture out in daylight without risking their lives—although they will give off a peculiar sparkling effect in sunlight. They can't fly, don't transform into bats, and don't rest in coffins. Though *Twilight* is intense, it is ultimately a romance, not a horror story; there are no graphic, violent scenes. "I do like to say it's a vampire book for people who don't like vampire books," Meyer commented.

A Series Emerges: "The Twilight Saga"

When Meyer had finished her original story, she still couldn't stop thinking about her characters. She wrote three different epilogues to the story, each more than 100 pages long. Realizing there was more she wanted to say about Edward and Bella, Meyer began to expand one of her epilogues into a full-length sequel, which she called "Forever Dawn." At that point, her first novel *Twilight* was still "Forks," a private work that only a handful of people had read. Meyer intended "Forever Dawn" as a birthday present for her sister Emily. When she was about 300 pages into writing "Forever Dawn," however, her life was turned upside down by the news of her book deal and the impending publication of *Twilight*.

> "Let me say that I do believe in true love. But I also deeply believe in the complexity, variety, and downright insanity of love. A lucky person loves hundreds of people in their lives, all in different ways.... The bottom line is that you have to choose who you're going to commit to—that's the foundation of love, not a lack of other options."

Little, Brown wanted at least two sequels to *Twilight,* but there was a problem: *Twilight* was being marketed as a young-adult book, and "Forever Dawn" didn't fit into the young-adult formula. In "Forever Dawn," Meyer had skipped past the conclusion of Bella's high-school years and written about a later part of her life. She knew she'd have to write a completely different story for Little, Brown—one that picked up directly after the conclusion of *Twilight*. She finished "Forever Dawn" and gave it to her sister as planned, then plunged into work on the official sequel, called *New Moon*. With the publication of *New Moon* and the following sequels, *Eclipse* and *Breaking Dawn,* the series became known as "The Twilight Saga."

New Moon

Writing the first book had been an act of pure joy, fun, and personal satisfaction for the author. Writing *New Moon* was an entirely different experience. "I knew enough about the editing process to know that there were painful changes ahead; the parts I loved now might not make the final cut," Meyer explained. "I was going to have to rethink and revise and rework. This made it very hard to put the words down, and I had a horrible feeling much like stage fright the whole time I was writing." Although the process of creating a sequel awaited by millions of eager readers was very difficult, Meyer felt it helped her to grow as a writer. It also provided an opportunity for her to give more depth to her characters.

Edward is absent from much of *New Moon.* Fearing that his presence brings too much danger to his beloved Bella, he has traveled far from her, at great risk to himself. Bella is devastated by his disappearance. The title of the book refers to the darkest point in the moon's cycle, a symbolic reference to this, the darkest period in Bella's life. With Edward lost to her, Bella develops a friendship with Jacob Black, a classmate who is part of the Quileute tribe. He tells Bella the tribe's legends, which say that its people descend-

New Moon *built on the success of* Twilight, *bringing more fans to the work.*

ed from wolves that were transformed into humans by a sorcerer. Jacob becomes Bella's protector when she is menaced by a vampire from a dangerous coven, whose presence causes Jacob to shape-shift into a huge werewolf. Released in September 2006, *New Moon* spent more than 25 weeks at the top of the *New York Times* bestseller list.

Eclipse

The publication of *Eclipse,* the third installment of the series, was eagerly awaited by the ever-growing ranks of "Twilight Saga" fans. Published in August 2007, the book sold 150,000 copies on the first day it was released. In *Eclipse,* Bella's high school graduation is approaching. While most students her age are concerned with choices about colleges or careers, Bella must make vital decisions on matters that may influence the course of a war between vampires and werewolves. Her choices will involve life and death and whether to remain human or become a vampire. Ultimately, she must choose between Edward and Jacob, which places them in competition, but the two rivals work together to try to save Bella when she is placed in harm's way.

A scene from the movie Eclipse, *due to be released in 2010, to be followed by* Breaking Dawn *in 2011.*

Some fans were dismayed by the growing relationship between Bella and Jacob. Bella had been portrayed as deeply in love with Edward, and fans disliked the idea that Bella could even consider a relationship with Jacob. But Meyer defended Bella: "First of all, let me say that I do believe in true love. But I also deeply believe in the complexity, variety, and downright insanity of love. A lucky person loves hundreds of people in their lives, all in different ways, family love, friendship love, romantic love, all in so many shades and depths. I don't think you lose your ability—or right—to have true love by loving more than one person.... The bottom line is that you have to choose who you're going to commit to—that's the foundation of love, not a lack of other options."

Reviewer Janis Flint-Ferguson wrote in *Kliatt* that *Eclipse,* like Meyer's first two books, "is hard to put down as it draws the reader into heart-pounding gothic romance tinged with mythic horror." Another reviewer, Anne Rouyer, commented in *School Library Journal* that "Meyer knows what her fans want: thrills, chills, and a lot of romance, and she delivers on all counts."

Breaking Dawn

Meyer's original deal with Little, Brown had been for three books, but with "The Twilight Saga" such a runaway success, the publisher was happy to extend the series with a fourth volume. At 12:01 a.m. on August 2, 2008, *Breaking Dawn* was released. Midnight parties were held at bookstores, with excited fans standing in line for hours to be able to get their hands on a copy of the book the instant it was available. Approximately 1.3 million copies were sold on the very first day *Breaking Dawn* came out.

The plot of *Breaking Dawn* sees Bella married. She soon becomes pregnant with a very unique, supernatural child, but the pregnancy is extremely dangerous to her. With this kind of storyline, *Breaking Dawn* is "darker and more mature than the previous titles" in "The Twilight Saga," according to Cara von Wrangel in a review for *School Library Journal.* Some fans weren't pleased with the plot, but as Meyer pointed out, any book with such a large, passionate audience would draw some negative response along with the positive.

Commenting on her decision to write a story about marriage and child-birth—subjects that might seem less appealing to her readers than high-school romance—Meyer said the following: "To me, the story was realistic. Things do change, you do grow up, and the world changes," she explained. "I wanted to see reality, and the reality is that things don't fade to black when you get married." *Breaking Dawn* provided closure to Bella's story, but the plot also left possibilities for new stories set in "The Twilight Saga" universe.

"I didn't realize the books would appeal to people so broadly," Meyer remarked. "I think some of it's because Bella is an everygirl. She's not a hero.... She doesn't always have to be cool, or wear the coolest clothes ever. She's normal. And there aren't a lot of girls in literature that are normal."

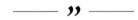

Throughout the creation of "The Twilight Saga," Meyer's busy imagination had driven her to begin rewriting the events from Edward's perspective, instead of Bella's. Initially, she only meant to do one chapter in this way, just as an exercise, but as usual, her imagination carried her further. She called the Edward-narrated story "Midnight Sun" and considered publishing it someday. Late in August 2008, Meyer was horrified to learn that a rough draft of "Midnight Sun" was being widely posted on the Internet. She had never intended the pages to be seen by the general public and was very upset. She responded by putting the draft up on her own Web site so that curious fans could read it there instead of on sites that had violated copyright laws by posting it. She also made a statement that she was putting the "Midnight Sun" project on hold indefinitely.

There was more excitement to come in 2008, when the film version of *Twilight* was released. Directed by Catherine Hardwicke, it featured Robert Pattinson as Edward, Kristen Stewart as Bella, and Taylor Lautner as Jacob. Meyer even appeared in the film, in a non-speaking role as a customer in a Forks diner. Fans flocked to see the movie, many of them dressing like their favorite characters for the occasion and returning for multiple viewings. *Twilight* was the No. 1 movie at the box office when it was released, with nearly $70 million in ticket sales on that weekend alone. It earned more than $380 million in box-office receipts during its run in theaters worldwide.

Excitement was just as high for the film sequel, *New Moon,* which was released in 2009. *New Moon* shattered the record for most money earned by a movie on its opening day, bringing in $72.7 million on opening day, more than $142 million over the opening weekend, and over $700 million at theaters. Fans are eagerly awaiting the movie versions of *Eclipse*, due out in June 2010, and *Breaking Dawn*, tentatively scheduled for 2011. Industry insiders have suggested that the final book, the longest book in "The Twilight Saga" series, may be broken in two and made into two movies. In another re-creation of this world, the original book in the series, *Twilight*, is being published as a graphic novel, with drawings by illustrator Young Kim. *Twilight: The Graphic Novel, Volume 1* is scheduled to be published in 2010.

"Twilight Saga" Mania

"The Twilight Saga" books appeal to fans of all ages and both genders, but younger teenage girls form the core of its fans. Often referring to themselves as "Twilighters," the vampire-obsessed girls are passionately interested in everything to do with "The Twilight Saga" books, movies, and author. They often define themselves as members of "Team Edward" or "Team Jacob" to show which character they're more devoted to. They have waited for hours in lines to get copies of the books on the day of their release, to have books signed by Meyer, or to be among the first to see the movie versions. They write their own fan-fiction based on the characters and listen to "Twilight Saga"-themed music. When special "Twilight Saga" prom parties were held with Meyer in attendance, tickets sold out within an hour after going on sale. "The Twilight Saga" books have sold some 70 million copies in total, and have been translated into more than 30 languages.

Meyer is very appreciative of all the fans who are so loyal to her work. "They have the best questions, and they're so into the stories," she said.

Meyer at the 2009 premiere of New Moon *with some of her dedicated fans.*

"You really can't write for a better audience. I say to all other authors: if you're not writing for teenage girls, you're missing out on a lot of love." Little, Brown has sent Meyer out on many tours to promote her work, and she has tried her best to keep in contact with her readers. Although the huge volume of mail she receives makes it impossible for her to answer every letter personally, she uses her Web site to provide fans with up-to-date information about what's going on with her and her work.

Meyer does have some detractors who find fault with her writing style. To such criticism, she responded: "I don't think I'm a writer; I think I'm a storyteller. The words aren't always perfect." Reflecting on the popularity of "The Twilight Saga," Meyer said: "I didn't realize the books would appeal to people so broadly. I think some of it's because Bella is an everygirl. She's not a hero.… She doesn't always have to be cool, or wear the coolest clothes ever. She's normal. And there aren't a lot of girls in literature that are normal."

Meyer is a quiet person who was happy with her life before she became a publishing celebrity. After a few whirlwind years of appearances at bookstores, special parties, concerts, and on national television programs to support "The Twilight Saga," she announced she would be stepping away from the media limelight for a while. She hoped to recapture some of her privacy and to get time to work on new writing projects. "Look, I'm not just a vampire girl," she said. "I can do other worlds."

Beyond "The *Twilight Saga*"

Meyer's first book outside "The Twilight Saga" was *The Host,* a science-fiction novel released in 2008. *The Host* is not considered a young-adult book, but Meyer's fans of all ages were eager to read it. It debuted at the top of the *New York Times* bestseller list and remained on the list for 26 weeks. *The Host* concerns a time when most of Earth has been taken over by alien invaders, called Souls, who inhabit human bodies. The host humans appear to go about their daily routines as usual, but once a Soul takes over, their human personalities cease to exist and their minds no longer function. The Souls have resolved many global problems, but there are still some renegade humans who want control of the planet.

> "If you love to write, then write. Don't let your goal be having a novel published, let your goal be enjoying your stories. However, if you finish your story and you want to share it, be brave about it. Don't doubt your story's appeal…. If I would have realized that the stories in my head would be as intriguing to others as they were to me, I would probably have started writing sooner. Believe in your own taste."

A showdown of sorts takes place within the body of Melanie Stryder, a human who is still without a Soul. She is what the aliens consider a rare, "wild" human, and as such, she is hunted down and taken into captivity. Her body is assigned to an experienced Soul called Wanderer, but when Wanderer inhabits Melanie's form, she finds that Melanie will not relinquish control of her mind. Instead, Melanie starts to exert control over Wanderer, filling the Soul's mind with thoughts of Jared, the man she loves. Jared is in hiding, and it is Wanderer's job to track him down. With Melanie's influence, however, Wanderer begins to have difficulty with her assignment. Things become even more complicated when Wanderer becomes attracted to Ian, another rebel human. Reviewing the book for *Library Journal,* Jane Jorgenson said Meyer succeeded in "blending science fiction and romance in a way that has never worked so well."

When asked by young writers how to achieve success, Meyer has given this advice: "If you love to write, then write. Don't let your goal be having a novel published, let your goal be enjoying your stories. However, if you finish your story and you want to share it, be brave about it. Don't doubt your story's appeal. If you are a good reader, and you know what is interesting, and your story is interesting to you, then trust in that. If I would have realized that the stories in my head would be as intriguing to others as they were to me, I would probably have started writing sooner. Believe in your own taste."

HOME AND FAMILY

Meyer and her family live in Cave Creek, Arizona, not far from where she grew up. Her parents still live nearby. Her husband formerly worked as an auditor at an accounting firm, but after Meyer became so busy touring and making appearances to support *Twilight* and its sequels, he quit his job so that one of them could be home to take care of their sons. The boys, Gabe, Seth, and Eli, were born in 1997, 2000, and 2002, respectively. Meyer is still a member of the Mormon church, which she calls "a huge influence on who I am and my perspective on the world."

FAVORITE BOOKS AND MUSIC

Meyer is an avid reader of all kinds of fiction, but she has named science fiction author Orson Scott Card and fantasy writer Terry Brooks as two of her favorite modern novelists. She likes all kinds of music, and a couple of her favorite groups are Linkin Park and Muse.

WRITINGS

The Host, 2008

"The Twilight Saga"

Twilight, 2005
New Moon, 2006
Eclipse, 2007
Breaking Dawn, 2008

HONORS AND AWARDS

Editor's Choice Selection (*New York Times*): 2005, for *Twilight*
Top Ten Best Books for Young Adults (American Library Association): 2005, for *Twilight*
Top Ten Books for Reluctant Readers (American Library Association): 2005, for *Twilight*

Most Promising New Authors of the Year (*Publishers Weekly*): 2005
Best Books of the Year (*Publishers Weekly*): 2005, for *Twilight*
Teen Choice Book of the Year Award: 2009, for *Breaking Dawn*
Children's Choice Author of the Year Award: 2009

FURTHER READING

Periodicals

Current Biography Yearbook, 2008
Entertainment Weekly, July 18, 2008, pp.22, 28
New York Times, Aug. 2, 2008, p.B7
New York Times Book Review, Aug. 12, 2007, p.19
Newsweek, Aug. 4, 2008, p.63
Publishers Weekly, July 18, 2005, p.207
School Library Journal, Oct. 2005, pp.37, 166; Oct. 2007, p.160; Oct. 2008, p.154
Time, May 5, 2008, p.49; Sep.1, 2008, p.4
USA Today, May 6, 2008, p.D7; July 31, 2008, p.D1

ADDRESS

Stephenie Meyer
Author Mail
Little, Brown and Company
237 Park Avenue
New York, NY 10017

WORLD WIDE WEB SITE

http://www.stepheniemeyer.com

Keke Palmer 1993-

American Actress and Singer
Star of the Film *Akeelah and the Bee* and the
Television Show "True Jackson, VP"

BIRTH

Lauren Keyana "Keke" Palmer was born on August 26, 1993, in Robbins, Illinois, a suburb of Chicago. Her father, Lawrence, worked for a plastics manufacturing company, and her mother, Sharon, worked with autistic high-school students. Both of her parents were professional actors earlier in life. She has an older sister, Loreal, who came up with the nickname "Keke" when they were children. "[Loreal] had an imaginary friend named Keke when she was four and wanted that to be my name," explained Palmer. She also has a younger sister and brother, Lawrencia and Lawrence, who are twins.

YOUTH

Palmer showed early promise as an entertainer. At the age of five, she impressed her church choir by singing an impassioned rendition of the traditional hymn "Jesus Loves Me." "I probably wasn't really, really in the choir," she later clarified. "I would just be sitting there dancing or singing or something, and … they made me a little robe to fit in with the choir.… I knew I wanted to entertain." Palmer credits both her church and her parents with providing valuable support. "I think [my talent] comes from the encouragement my parents and my church gave me to follow my dreams and [their] telling me that I could achieve anything," she confided. "So, I've always felt confident and secure, and was able to be myself and to have a good time."

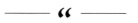

> *"I think [my talent] comes from the encouragement my parents and my church gave me to follow my dreams and [their] telling me that I could achieve anything," Palmer confided. "So, I've always felt confident and secure, and was able to be myself and to have a good time."*

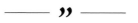

Palmer started acting when she was nine years old. "It was kind of spur of the moment. My dad was reading in the paper about *Lion King* auditions and asked me if I wanted to go," she recalled. "I auditioned and out of 400 kids … I made it down to the top 15. And then I was out. … I definitely got bit by the acting bug." In 2004 she made her film debut in *Barbershop 2: Back in Business,* the sequel to the hit 2002 comedy *Barbershop* starring rapper Ice Cube. The producers were so impressed with Palmer that they suggested she move to Los Angeles to be closer to the major film studios. Convinced of their daughter's chances at success in the entertainment industry, Palmer's parents moved the family to Duarte, a suburb of Los Angeles.

EDUCATION

Before moving to California, Palmer attended St. Benedict Catholic Elementary School in Blue Island, a suburb south of Chicago. "When I was in kindergarten all the way up to third grade, I was kind of an introvert," she disclosed. "I was a little bit more quiet in school than I was outside of

Palmer as Nikki Grady in Madea's Family Reunion, *shown with Tyler Perry as Madea.*

school." In third grade, she placed second in the spelling bee, but lost when she spelled the word "gorilla" with two R's and one L. "I'm not afraid, you know, to do good in school," she said. "[But] my friends back in Chicago … some of them were afraid to be smart and do good in school because people might think they're nerds.… I didn't struggle with anything like that."

Since becoming an actress, Palmer has studied independently and has attended school on the sets of her films and television shows. "I go to school Tuesdays and Thursdays, so all of those days in between I work and do the school work that they give me. And then I turn it in to my teacher and they make me take a test to make sure that no one did my schoolwork for me. After that, I'm done with that subject," she explained. Her favorite subject is English, and her least favorite is math. She plans to attend college in the future. "I'm thinking about going to Howard University and getting my master's at Yale. If acting doesn't work out, maybe I'll be an anesthesiologist.… All I have to do is get a little bit better in math and science."

CAREER HIGHLIGHTS

Palmer began auditioning for acting roles in Los Angeles, and within weeks she found herself in a Kmart commercial as well as episodes of the television dramas "Strong Medicine" and "Cold Case." She was also given a chance to shoot a pilot episode of a show called "Keke & Jamal" for the Disney Channel. The show was about a cranky old man who finds himself taking care of his two grandchildren, but Disney decided not to air the program. Little did Palmer realize that she would later have her own successful series.

Landing a Major Role

Palmer first gained widespread recognition with her performance in *The Wool Cap*, a Turner Network Television movie that premiered in 2004. Starring opposite esteemed actor William H. Macy, Palmer played Lou, the daughter of a drug addict living in a neglected New York City apartment building. Macy played Charlie Gigot, the manager of the building. After Lou's mom leaves her in Charlie's care and never returns, both characters end up helping each other grow as individuals. She earned a nomination for Outstanding Performance by a Female Actor from the Screen Actors Guild for the movie, becoming the youngest-ever nominee in that category. The honor came as a total surprise to 12-year-old Palmer: "I couldn't believe it at first. When my mom came to tell me, I was just sitting there [thinking], 'She's kidding me.'"

> "I was doubtful at first about doing some of the acting jobs because they were so big," Palmer confessed. "But as I got to another level I kind of realized, well, I've gotten this far. Maybe I am good enough. And that's what Akeelah thought when she got to the regional bee."

Over the next couple of years, Palmer appeared in a number of other television projects, including the hit shows "ER" and "Law & Order: Special Victims Unit." She also had a supporting role in filmmaker Tyler Perry's popular 2006 comedy *Madea's Family Reunion*. Palmer played Nikki Grady, a rebellious teenage runaway who has been in foster care most of her life and who joins Madea's family when the court orders Madea to take care of her.

Akeelah and the Bee

Palmer's major commercial and critical breakthrough came in 2006, when she starred in the acclaimed film *Akeelah and the Bee*. The plot concerns Akeelah Anderson, a middle-school student from an inner-city neighbor-

A scene from Akeelah and the Bee, *with Tanya, Akeelah's mother (Angela Bassett), Mr. Welch (Curtis Armstrong), Dr. Larabee (Laurence Fishburne), and Akeelah (Keke Palmer).*

hood in Los Angeles. When Akeelah wins the school's spelling bee, an English teacher named Dr. Joshua Larabee (played by Laurence Fishburne) suggests that she compete in the Scripps National Spelling Bee in Washington DC. Her widowed mother (played by actress Angela Bassett) is initially hesitant to let her participate, but she eventually agrees. In the end, Akeelah shares first prize with her former rival, a Chinese American boy named Dylan.

Palmer has remarked on the challenges of preparing for the role. "The script had words I didn't even know were real," she said with a laugh. She has related her own experiences as an actress to Akeelah's decision to compete at a national level. "I was doubtful at first about doing some of the acting jobs because they were so big," she confessed. "But as I got to another level I kind of realized, well, I've gotten this far. Maybe I am good enough. And that's what Akeelah thought when she got to the regional bee."

Akeelah and the Bee was a critical success, and Palmer was widely praised for her performance. "Palmer takes what could have been a conventional part in a feel-good movie to a higher level," raved Claudia Puig in *USA Today*. In *Variety*, critic Justin Chang argued that Palmer "movingly illuminates the pressures facing a girl caught between the ordinary and extraordinary." Palmer was honored with a Black Movie Award, a Black Reel Award, an NAACP Image Award, and a Young Artist Award for the role. At ShoWest, a prestigious tradeshow for owners of movie theaters, the judges created a special new award, the Rising Star of the Year Award, just for her.

Branching Out to Music

Akeelah and the Bee also afforded Palmer the opportunity to demonstrate her skills as a singer, featuring her vocal performance of the song "All My Girlz" on its soundtrack. Atlantic Records took note of her musical talent and offered her a record deal. Her debut album, *So Uncool,* was released in 2007. It contains four songs written by Palmer, including "Skin Deep," which addresses the importance of inner beauty rather than physical appearance. "I wrote that song for those people who are truly beautiful, but they just don't see it," she explained. Atlantic Records has described the songs on the album as "ranging from up-tempo R&B tracks to inspirational songs to youthful, fun material that kids can relate to." To promote *So Uncool,* Palmer toured with the WNBA and performed songs from the album at halftime.

Also in 2007, Palmer starred in the Disney Channel original movie *Jump In!* A musically oriented feature in the tradition of *High School Musical, Jump In!* is the story of Mary (played by Palmer) who convinces her male friend Izzy (played by Corbin Bleu) to join her competitive jump-rope team. Izzy discovers that he is a natural at jump rope, but worries what his father and friends will think when they find out. With 8.2 million viewers tuning in, *Jump In!* set a Disney Channel record for largest audience for an original television movie premiere. The movie's soundtrack was also a hit, and featured two new songs sung by Palmer.

The Longshots

In 2008 Palmer got the chance to portray a genuine trailblazer when she landed the lead role opposite Ice Cube in *The Longshots,* a movie directed by Fred Durst of the band Limp Bizkit. *The Longshots* is the true story of Jasmine Plummer (played by Palmer), an Illinois teenager who became the first female quarterback to play in a Pop Warner football tournament. The Pop Warner Little Scholars is the country's biggest youth football and cheerleading organization, and Jasmine Plummer led the Harvey Colts of Illinois to the Pop Warner Super Bowl in 2003. The movie was well received, with *Variety* critic Joe Leydon claiming, "Cube and Palmer show engaging sincerity and impeccable professionalism.… And the climax provides a welcome touch of realism that recalls the original *Rocky.*"

Jasmine (Palmer) with Curtis Plummer (Ice Cube, center) in a scene from The Longshots.

Ironically, Plummer lived about five minutes from Palmer's suburban Chicago home when the events in the movie took place. The two girls got a chance to meet during filming, and Palmer was drawn to the positive message of Plummer's story. "What mainly interested me in the role was that it was so inspirational," she stated. "I thought it would really motivate young girls to pursue their dreams." Although she had no previous experience playing football, she learned how to handle the ball onscreen. "I practiced for about four months, getting my arm ready, and then learning the footwork," she said. "I was even better than some of the boys."

"True Jackson, VP"

Palmer's most high-profile role came in 2008 when the Nickelodeon Network hired her to star in her own television series, "True Jackson, VP." The show revolves around a teenage girl named True Jackson who becomes vice president of a billion-dollar fashion company. As she gets to know the fashion world, she realizes that it is a lot like high school. The show was a major success right from the start, becoming the largest debut in Nickelodeon's history. Palmer felt like she really connected with the role and the audience. "I really wanted to get [this part]," she admitted. "I do a lot of movies that are drama related and wanted [this] so my own peers could

True Jackson (Palmer) with Lulu Johnson (Ashley Argota) and Ryan Laserbeam (Matt Shively) in a scene from "True Jackson, VP."

see me as someone just like them. They could maybe understand me a little bit better, and I could be closer to them." Her work on the show impressed her bosses as much as her fans. "Keke is totally natural," Nickelodeon's Marjorie Cohn told *USA Today.* "She's bubbly, she's self-confident, but she's not conceited.... She's a real kid and a really nice person, and I think that just comes across on camera."

The success of "True Jackson, VP" led to the launching of a clothing line based on the show. Designed by Jane Siskin and sold at Walmart, the Mad Style by True Jackson line consists of a wide range of clothing and accessories for young girls. Although Siskin was the official designer, Palmer had plenty of input. "They showed me the first samples and I was able to say what I liked and what I didn't like," she explained. Commenting on her own personal sense of style, she declared: "I like to be edgy but I also make sure the look is still sweet and young."

Recent Work

In addition to her hit television series, Palmer appeared in *Madea Goes to Jail,* the 2009 Tyler Perry film. She again appeared as Nikki Grady, whom Madea has taken in as a foster child. She also appeared in the 2009 film *Shrink,* a dark comedy starring Academy Award-winner Kevin Spacey. He plays Henry Carter, a depressed psychiatrist attempting to solve his own issues while tending to his patients. One of these patients is Jemma (played by Palmer), a troubled teen who loves films. Although *Shrink* got mixed reviews, critics lauded her skills as an actress. "Keke Palmer's performance as a high school-age film nut provides some welcome grounding in reality," claimed John Anderson of *Variety*.

HOME AND FAMILY

Palmer has a close relationship with her older sister, Loreal, who co-wrote some of the tracks on *So Uncool* and also provided background vocals, along with her younger twin siblings. The family also has a pet dog, a lhasa apso named Rusty. She has cited her parents as the most inspirational people in her life. "They travel with me wherever I go and they are a huge blessing. They have truly inspired me to be the best I can be and have helped me to become a strong person."

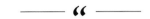

"Keke is totally natural," raved Nickelodeon's Marjorie Cohn. *"She's bubbly, she's self-confident, but she's not conceited.... She's a real kid and a really nice person, and I think that just comes across on camera."*

HOBBIES AND OTHER INTERESTS

Palmer is active in several charitable causes, including the Girl Scouts and the mentor program It's Cool to Be Smart. "I try to tell the students to never give up on your dreams," she stated. In her spare time, she enjoys reading. "One of my favorite books is *A Wrinkle in Time* by Madeleine L'Engle," she said. "When you finish reading a book, you feel like you've accomplished a great thing." In addition, she likes going to the movies, talking on the phone, playing video games, and window-shopping with her friends. Her favorite foods include Chicago-style pizza and bacon cheeseburgers.

SELECTED CREDITS

Television and Movies

Barbershop 2: Back in Business, 2004
The Wool Cap, 2004 (TV movie)
Akeelah and the Bee, 2006
Madea's Family Reunion, 2006

Jump In! 2007 (TV movie)
The Longshots, 2008
"True Jackson, VP," 2008- (TV series)
Madea Goes to Jail, 2009
Shrink, 2009

Recordings

So Uncool, 2007

HONORS AND AWARDS

Black Movie Award (Film Life): 2006, Outstanding Performance by an Actress in a Leading Role, for *Akeelah and the Bee*
Special Award (ShoWest Convention, USA): 2006, Rising Star of the Year
Black Reel Award (Foundation for the Advancement of African-Americans in Film): 2007, Best Actress, for *Akeelah and the Bee*
Image Award (NAACP): 2007, Outstanding Actress in a Motion Picture, for *Akeelah and the Bee*; 2009, Outstanding Performance in a Youth/Children's Program—Series or Special, for "True Jackson, VP"
Young Artist Award (Young Artist Foundation): 2007, Best Performance in a Feature Film—Leading Young Actress, for *Akeelah and the Bee*

FURTHER READING

Books

Bloom, Ronny. *Keke Palmer: A True Star; An Unauthorized Biography,* 2009 (juvenile)
Brooks, Riley. *All Access: Keke Palmer; Unauthorized Bio,* 2009 (juvenile)

Periodicals

Cosmo Girl, Aug. 2008, p.67
Ebony, Dec. 2007, p.42
Jet, May 1, 2006, p.58; Apr. 26, 2009
Sports Illustrated, Mar. 17, 2008, p.22
Teen Vogue, Aug. 2009, p.46
TV Guide, Jan. 19, 2009
USA Today, Apr. 27, 2006, p.D5; May 5, 2009, p.D2

Online Articles

http://www.atlanticrecords.com/kekepalmer
    (Atlantic Records, "Keke Palmer," undated)

http://www.ew.com
  (Entertainment Weekly, "Keke Palmer: The Next Big Thing," Nov. 28, 2008)
http://www.mtv.com/movies/person/382096/personmain.jhtml
  (MTV, "Keke Palmer," undated)
http://www.people.com
  (People, "Nickelodeon's Keke Palmer Celebrates Sweet 16," Aug. 26, 2009, articles archive)

ADDRESS

Keke Palmer
Nickelodeon Network
1515 Broadway
New York, NY 10036

WORLD WIDE WEB SITES

http://www.kekepalmer.com
http://www.nick.com/shows/truejacksonvp
http://www.myspace.com/therealkekepalmer

PARAMORE
Jeremy Davis 1985-
Josh Farro 1987-
Zac Farro 1990-
Hayley Williams 1988-
Taylor York 1989-
American Punk-Pop-Rock Band
Creators of *RIOT!* and *brand new eyes*

EARLY YEARS

The Tennessee-based rock band Paramore, whose music has been described as alternative rock, punk-pop, and emo, consists of five members: vocalist Hayley Williams, guitarist Joshua Farro, drummer Zachary Farro, bassist Jeremy Davis, and rhythm guitarist Taylor York. Most of the band members were still in their teens when the group recorded their first album, and many of their fans fall into the same age group. As the group has matured, however, they have expanded their appeal as well as their success.

———— **"** ————

When they were just starting out, the members of Paramore shared their love of music. "Back then, I guess we were all thinking, after school we'll go to the house and practice," Williams recalled. "It was what we loved to do for fun, and still do! I don't think any of us really knew this would turn out to be what it's become."

———— **"** ————

Lead singer Hayley Nichole Williams was born on December 27, 1988. She moved from Meridian, Mississippi, to Franklin, Tennessee, in her early teens after her parents divorced. When she had trouble fitting in at a local public school, she enrolled at a private school, where she met fellow music lovers Josh and Zac Farro. They formed Paramore while she was still in high school. Because of the band's touring schedule, she finished her high school diploma through an internet home schooling program.

Guitarist Joshua Neil Farro was born on September 29, 1987, and grew up in Franklin, Tennessee. The second of five children, he learned to play guitar by watching his father teach his older brother. His next youngest sibling, drummer Zachary Wayne Farro, was born on June 4, 1990. Like Williams, he was still in school when the band formed—in fact, he was only 12. As its youngest member, he also completed his high school education through the same internet home schooling program as Williams.

Less is known about the childhoods of the other members of Paramore, although they also grew up around Franklin, Tennessee. Bassist Jeremy Clayton Davis was born on February 8, 1985. He is the oldest member of Paramore by a couple of years, and he had more experience as a musician before joining the band. He had even played as a session musician in Nashville studios. Guitarist Taylor Benjamin York was born on December 17, 1989. Although York was not an original member of Paramore, he had been involved with the band from its early days, co-writing the occasional song and performing live with the group on tour. He joined Paramore's official lineup in June 2009.

FORMING THE BAND

An early version of Paramore was formed around 2002 in Franklin, Tennessee. Brothers Zac and Josh Farro formed a band and asked Williams, the new girl at their school, if she would like to join. "They were the first people I met who were as passionate about music as I was," Williams recalled, and the three met to play together and listen to bands. Williams soon brought in bassist Davis, with whom she had played in a funk cover band. Davis, an experienced musician, was startled to arrive at the first rehearsal and discover that the drummer was only 12 years old. "I had very, very, very little faith in everyone in the band because of their age," he admitted. He already knew Williams had vocal potential, however, so he stuck around and was amazed by his new band mates' creative abilities. "I remember thinking, 'This is not going to work because this kid is way too young,' but that first day of practice was amazing. I knew we were onto something."

The band, now composed of the two Farro brothers, Williams, and Davis, later added a rhythm guitarist, Jason Bynum. They soon began playing high school talent shows and local rock clubs. By 2004 they were known as Paramore and had begun touring the southeast, often driven around by Williams's parents. "Back then, I guess we were all thinking, after school we'll go to the house and practice," Williams noted. "It was what we loved to do for fun, and still do! I don't think any of us really knew this would turn out to be what it's become."

It wasn't long before the group was attracting industry notice. The Agency Group, a music management company, signed them when Williams was just 14. "I was impressed by her raw talent at that young age," booking agent Ken Fermaglieli told *Billboard* magazine. "I knew when I met her that there was a star there. She knew exactly what she was doing, how she wanted to do it, and she had a plan." The company helped Paramore book gigs all around the southeast region. While performing in Florida, they were seen by independent label Fueled By Ramen and signed in April 2005. The label had also broken such punk-flavored acts as Jimmy Eat World, Fall Out Boy, Gym Class Heroes, and Panic! At the Disco, and they thought Paramore was a natural fit. "Even though they were very young, I could see there was something special there," label president John Janick told *Billboard*, "and I could look down the road and see them playing much bigger venues." Their deal with the label—known as a "360-degree" deal—meant they would share touring and merchandise revenue with their label in exchange for extra promotional support and time to grow a fan base on the road.

Paramore's debut album, All We Know Is Falling.

CAREER HIGHLIGHTS

Developing an Audience

Paramore recorded its first album, *All We Know Is Falling,* and released it in late summer 2005. Williams and Josh Farro co-wrote all of the album's songs, most of which dealt with relationships. Davis had left the band for a short period after they began recording—he returned shortly after the album was released—and his departure inspired the song "All We Know." Williams noted that the single "Emergency" was inspired by the failure of her parents' marriage and that although the band was young, they could still write meaningful songs. "I know we are a lot younger than even a lot of our fans, and it's a constant fight to get people to take us seriously," the singer said. "I grew up with my parents fighting a lot and the guys in the band grew up with similar situations and anyone can see what love isn't, no matter what their age."

With songs that combined mid-tempo verses with fast-paced power choruses, *All We Know Is Falling* found an audience of mostly younger fans. The group's pop-punk sensibilities and Williams's powerhouse vocals drew comparisons to such hard-driving popular artists as Evanescence and Avril Lavigne. The album drew some favorable notices from critics, including comments from a *New York Times* writer that Williams's "impressive" vocals made her "a potential star." Although the group made videos for singles "Pressure," "Emergency," and "All We Know," the record had only modest sales, not enough to make the Billboard 200 Album chart.

Their label wasn't alarmed. Their plan was to grow a fan base through live shows, and Paramore set out on tour in summer 2005. They appeared at New Jersey's Bamboozle Festival as well as several dates on the Vans Warped Tour. They were on a side stage that focused on female-fronted groups; the band had to help assemble the stage and only played before

"Paramore realizes the punk-pop formula with such guileless fervor that it becomes entertaining in itself," a reviewer for **Stylus Magazine** *observed, adding that "as punk more extravagantly flirts with pop and pop explores short, sharp rock songs, Paramore finds a comfortable place between the two."*

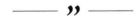

40 or 50 people, but soon their high-energy performances began to draw in bigger audiences. Bynum left the group that year, replaced by Hunter Lamb on rhythm guitar, and still the group continued to tour. In 2006 they began playing some headlining dates at small venues around the United States, including New York City.

Paramore rejoined the Vans Warped Tour in 2006, this time on a bigger stage. They also began touring internationally. The time away from home was challenging for the young performers, but the band felt the experience and exposure was worth it. "We all miss home sometimes and wonder what we'd be doing if we weren't sitting in a van traveling to the next venue," Williams noted, "but at the same time, some kid might be sitting in class wondering how it would be to be sitting in a van traveling to the next venue. We are all doing what we love and don't regret any of it." By fall 2006, *All We Know Is Falling* made an appearance on Billboard's Heatseekers Album chart.

Breaking out with *RIOT!*

In early 2007, only a few months before their second album was due to be released, Lamb left the group to get married. Paramore announced the band would continue as quartet for the near future, even as they prepared to support their new CD. *RIOT!* was produced by David Bendeth and covered many of the same themes as their first album, although the group branched out a bit musically. "For us, the title *RIOT!* literally means an unbridled outburst of emotions," Williams explained. "When we were writing, it seemed our thought and emotions were coming out so fast that we couldn't control them. It felt like there was a riot within us. So the album takes our passion to a new level; it's just all raw energy." The CD produced several successful singles that charted on the Billboard Hot 100, including "Misery Business," "crushcrushcrush," and "That's What You Get." The album received positive attention from critics, too. "Paramore realizes the punk-pop formula with such guileless fervor that it becomes entertaining in itself," a reviewer for *Stylus Magazine* observed, adding that "as punk more extravagantly flirts with pop and pop explores short, sharp rock songs, Paramore finds a comfortable place between the two."

Paramore continued touring to support the album, this time playing the main stage on some 2007 Vans Warped dates. Their videos began to get airplay on MTV, and a partnership with retailer Hot Topic led to Paramore T-shirt/download bundles being featured in the store. People were beginning to take notice of the group, helped along by Williams's powerful vocals, colorful hairstyles (usually involving some bright shade of orange or red), and sense of style. Having a female singer front the band helped them stand out among all the other punk-inspired rock groups, something that inspired Williams. "I don't think so much about the fact I'm a girl fronting the band; it's just there's not a lot of girls fronting bands in our genre," she explained. "It's just how it is. It's really motivating to me." In summer 2007 *Entertainment Weekly* named Paramore one of the Ten Most Exciting Artists of the year, and *RIOT!* was well on its way to gaining platinum (million-selling) status.

The year 2008 provided other milestones for the group. They kept touring, including two months as co-headliners with their idols Jimmy Eat World. *RIOT!* officially earned platinum status in July, and the group earned a Grammy nomination for best new artist (they lost to singer Amy Winehouse). They performed at the 2008 MTV Video Awards, where "crushcrushcrush" was nominated for Best Rock Video and also won the 2008 MTVu Woodie of the Year Award. They picked up two Teen Choice Awards, for choice Rock Group and Rock Song for "crushcrushcrush." They were also nominated for Breakthrough Artist at the 2008 American Music Awards.

Paramore in about 2007, when RIOT! *was released.*

Their increased visibility also brought out skeptics who wondered whether the young band was really in control of their music or whether they were manufactured, like some other teen performers. Band members were

111

quick to defend themselves. Zac Farro disputed that idea by recalling his childhood pudginess, since outgrown. "Would a label put us together if I was 11 years old and weighed, like, 400 pounds?" he asked. "They wouldn't be like, 'Let's get that guy!'" Davis added that youth had nothing to do with talent. "Some of the ideas that come out of Josh and Zac and Hayley's heads—it astounds me at times, because I remember how young they are," the bassist said. "I just feel like they're super-creative." Williams noted that one advantage Paramore had was that they wrote all their own songs. "It's really important for an artist to believe what they're talking about," the singer remarked. "I've gone through everything I wrote about, and I hope that gives people an emotional connection to the music."

Working through Growing Pains

With the increased media attention came increased pressure. Rumors surfaced that Paramore was breaking up after they cancelled some tour dates in Europe in early 2008, citing "internal issues" that needed to be resolved within the band. While some observers speculated that there was friction because Williams was getting more media attention than the rest of the band, the singer explained to MTV that the group was merely exhausted after more than a year on the road. "Touring really got to us. We still love it with all our hearts, but it takes a toll mentally and physically. But we just needed time with our friends and family, and just [to relax] and basically refuel." The break made them eager to keep working together. As bassist Davis commented afterward, "things haven't been this good in a very long time as far as our relationships with each other." "All of us are looking forward to getting back in the studio," Williams added. "That will be amazing for us—therapeutic, even. It will be great to have time set aside to just be a band, apart from the hype and insanity."

It wasn't long before Paramore was back on the road, making occasional appearances on the Vans Warped Tour and headlining several dates, including a performance at Central Park in New York City. Reviewing the concert on *The Blender.com,* Ryan Dombal called the band "stupendously tight and anything but amateur live." While the band received a lot of press for their

Paramore performing live in Hollywood in 2008.

youth, Dombal added that *RIOT!* "is one of the best mainstream rock albums of the decade" and that Paramore is "making vital music that their young followers can grow into naturally." The live CD/DVD of the tour, *Final RIOT!*, appeared in late 2008 and sold 500,000 copies within four months to be certified gold. The DVD captured the energy of the band's live shows, where the charismatic Williams commanded the stage despite her petite frame. Her youthful appeal led to some acting offers, but Williams turned them down. "I love the stage, the sweaty sickness, dancing and screaming," she said. "I'm not sure I'd fit on the big screen."

Nevertheless, Paramore found a way to get involved with one of the biggest films of 2008. They recorded two songs for the soundtrack to *Twilight,* the vampire love story based on the bestselling book of the same name by Stephenie Meyer (for more information on Meyer, see p. 77 of this issue). Williams had fallen in love with the *Twilight* books while on tour, and she asked Paramore's management to arrange for the band to contribute music to the movie. "We kinda fought tooth and nail to make sure we could be part of the soundtrack," Williams said. Featuring two Paramore songs, "Decode" and "I Caught Myself," the *Twilight* soundtrack album was No. 1 in its first week of release with over 165,000 copies sold and eventually sold more than two million copies. "Decode" was the lead single from the CD and became the group's first Top 40 single, hitting No. 33. The video for "Decode" earned a MTV Video Music Award nomination for best rock video, as well as an MTV Movie Award nomination for best song from a movie. The single also brought the group its second Grammy nomination: a songwriters' award for Williams, York, and Josh Farro, for Best Song Written for Motion Picture, Television, or Other Visual Media.

The band went through more personnel changes in June 2009. Guitarist Taylor York, who had frequently worked with the band as a songwriter and touring performer since its founding in 2004, was announced as an official member and joined band members for their next recording session. They went into the studio with producer Rob Cavallo, who had worked with such superstars as Green Day, Kid Rock, and Avril Lavigne. He helped Paramore expand the group's sound. As Zac Farro noted, "Our heavier songs are a lot bigger. I really think they capture that live sound. Our ballads are a lot more mature. I think we took a slight risk." Many of Williams's lyrics dealt with the group's conflicts, so she was a bit leery to share them with the band. "I was kind of embarrassed and didn't know how they would take it," she revealed. "But once all those words were out on the table, it gave us the opportunity to hash through our problems and internal struggles that we had been facing." She added that "once that was done, it was back to the old us and back to the old reasons why we started a band and why we wanted to play music together." If you listen closely to the album, the singer suggested, "you can hear the progression of songs go from angry and spiteful to super-hopeful and positive."

brand new eyes

While the group members hoped their expanded sound would appeal to a wider audience, even they were surprised by the performance of *brand new eyes* when it debuted in October 2009. It sold over 175,000 copies in its first week alone and entered the Billboard 200 chart at No. 2, behind Barbra

brand new eyes *features the band's current lineup: Jeremy Davis, Josh Farro, Zac Farro, Hayley Williams, and Taylor York.*

Streisand but ahead of new albums by Mariah Carey, Alice in Chains, and Madonna. The album charted at No. 1 in Ireland, Australia, New Zealand, and the United Kingdom, and the band sold out England's famous Wembley Stadium in eight hours. Fans weren't the only ones to take notice of the new album. Evan Lucy noted in *Billboard* that the album showed a "newfound maturity that makes for a compelling set of songs," while a *New York Times* contributor noted that the new album "broadened the band's dynamics without sacrificing momentum." The album produced the singles "Ignorance" and "Brick by Boring Brick." The video for the latter track was a special effects-laden, story-driven piece with no scenes of the band performing—a first for the group.

The year 2009 had other triumphs for the group. They were chosen by supergroup No Doubt to open for them on their 2009 comeback tour, a thrill for longtime fan Williams. She considered singer Gwen Stefani one of the few female role models in her genre, and Williams and Davis had covered the reggae-influenced group when they were in a funk cover band. In the fall of 2009 the group recorded an episode of "MTV Unplugged," bringing high energy to their set with only acoustic instruments. Headlining a show in Boston, the group "looked and sounded like a unified force, spring-loaded to deliver the kind of boisterous pop that defines summer soundtracks," Jonathan Perry remarked in the *Boston Globe*. The group also headlined MTV's first Ulalume Music Festival in the fall and was selected to co-headline New Jersey's Bamboozle Festival in 2010.

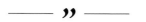

"Our faith is very important to us," Josh Farro remarked. "It's obviously going to come out in our music because if someone believes something then their worldview is going to come out in anything they do. But we're not out here to preach to kids, we're out here because we love music. We do believe that God has blessed us with an opportunity to be in a band and tour the world and we're going to use this gift to the full potential."

As awards season rolled around, Paramore found themselves in contention once again. They repeated as Teen Choice Award winners, taking home the 2009 awards for Choice Rock Group and for Choice Rock Track, for "Decode." They also won the 2010 People's Choice Award for Favorite Rock Band. Band members attributed their success to a lot of hard work. "It took a lot of sacrifice and years of touring and working our way from the ground up to get to this point," Williams stressed. "And even if it was all taken away from us tomorrow, every bit of it was worth it." They were also ready for any further successes that might come: "Maybe this record [*brand new eyes*] will be the one that has paparazzi following us around," the singer remarked. "But if there's anything I know more than anything else in the world, it's that I'm not gonna change for anyone. I just don't see the point."

The band credits their ability to avoid the usual pitfalls of musical stardom to their strong Christian beliefs. "Our faith is very important to us," Josh Farro remarked. "It's obviously going to come out in our music because if someone believes something then their worldview is going to come out in anything they do. But we're not out here to preach to kids, we're out here because we love music." He added, "We do believe that God has blessed us with an opportunity to be in a band and tour the world and we're going to use this gift to the full potential." While out on the road, the band avoids partying and enjoys watching movies and sightseeing instead, but they don't believe this makes them better than anyone else. As Williams explained, "I try to talk about struggles and imperfections and even questioning your faith at times. I don't have anything figured out that the next kid doesn't. It's the people who shove their faith down people's throats who create the stigma against artists with religious backgrounds."

Many people have asked Williams about her future plans, but she has no plans to go solo. "I love being in a band. I can't see myself singing alone and just being Hayley, you know. That would feel so weird." In fact, many attribute Paramore's success to the band members' ability to work together as a group to create their songs. Josh Farro comes up with music, sometimes a lyric or vocal line. He brings it to Williams, who builds lyrics and adds melodies. Then the rest of band fleshes out the arrangements and transitions. "There's something Hayley is able to draw out of me that I can't seem to do with anyone else," Josh Farro said about his songwriting partner. As long as the band keeps exploring music together, he added, "I don't really care how many records we sell." Williams expressed a similar sentiment: "I just want to feel like this is my band, this is awesome, I'm living the dream. If we can accomplish that together, there's nothing more that we can ask for." They'll keep making music together as long as they have devoted fans, many of whom correspond with the band on their web site and find comfort in Paramore's music. As Davis concluded, "I feel like, if we were ever to break up, we would be letting down all those kids. That's never even an option."

HOME AND FAMILY

As a popular band on tour, the members of Paramore get little time to spend at home. When they get a chance, however, they enjoy being with their families and friends back in Franklin, Tennessee. All of the band members are single and plan on devoting their time to the band in the near future.

FAVORITE MUSIC

Although the band has a variety of influences, they cite several groups as their favorites, including Jimmy Eat World, Death Cab for Cutie, Radiohead, mewithoutYou, Mum, Sigur Ros, and sunny day real estate.

HOBBIES AND OTHER INTERESTS

When the band gets a chance to enjoy some rare free time, their interests are pretty typical of young adults. They all enjoy hanging out with friends and family, and Josh and Jeremy enjoy movies. Taylor cites bicycling as a favorite activity, while Zac likes bowling. Hayley likes fashion, especially playing with hair and make-up; she has said that if she hadn't become a musician she would gone to cosmetology school.

RECORDINGS

All We Know Is Falling, 2005
RIOT!, 2007
The Final RIOT!, 2008 (live CD/DVD)
Twilight: Original Motion Picture Soundtrack, 2008 (contributor)
brand new eyes, 2009

HONORS AND AWARDS

Woodie Award (MTVu): 2008, for Woodie of the Year
Teen Choice Awards: 2008, for Choice Rock Group, and for Choice Rock Track, for "crushcrushcrush"; 2009, for Choice Rock Group, and for Choice Rock Track, for "Decode"
People's Choice Award: 2010, for Favorite Rock Band

FURTHER READING

Periodicals

Alternative Press, Oct. 11, 2007; Mar. 27, 2008; Oct. 13, 2009
Billboard, Oct. 6, 2007, p.18; Sep. 27, 2008, p.21; July 18, 2009, p.13; Sep. 18, 2009, p.36
Boston Globe, Oct. 18, 2009; Oct. 21, 2009
Houston Chronicle, May 30, 2009
Los Angeles Times, June 28, 2007, p.E4; May 10, 2009, p.E13
New York Times, Dec. 22, 2005, p.E1; Nov. 30, 2007, p.E23; Sep. 28, 2009, p.C3
Rolling Stone, Mar. 6, 2008, p.20; May 28, 2009, p.19; Oct. 1, 2009, p.34
San Jose Mercury News, Apr. 6, 2008
USA Today, Aug. 31, 2007, p.E10
Washington Post, Nov. 23, 2008, p.M2

Online Articles

http://www.theagencygroup.com
(The Agency Group Ltd., "Paramore," Oct. 2, 2009)

http://newsvote.bbc.co.uk
   (BBC News, "Talking Shop: Paramore," Feb. 6, 2008)
http://www.blender.com
   (The Blender, "Live: Paramore Are the Future," Sep. 1, 2008; "Collect
   Call from Paramore," Dec. 15, 2008)
http://www.fueledbyramen.com
   (Fueled by Ramen, "Paramore," Sep. 3, 2009)
http://www.mtv.com
   (MTV, "Paramore Exclusive: Band Addresses Breakup Rumors, 'Internal
   Issues,'" Mar. 14, 2008; "Paramore Battle Doubt, Each Other to Make
   New Album," May 19, 2009)
http://www.shockhound.com
   (Shockhound.com, "Paramore: Group Therapy," July 15, 2009)
http://www.soundthesirens.com
   (Sound the Sirens Magazine, "Paramore: Youth Gone Wild," Oct. 17,
   2005)
http://www.stylusmagazine.com
   (Stylus Magazine, "Paramore: Riot!," Aug. 13, 2007)

ADDRESSES

Paramore
Fueled By Ramen
PO Box 1803
Tampa, FL 33601

Paramore
The Official Paramore Fan Club
853 Broadway, 3rd Floor
New York, NY 10003

WORLD WIDE WEB SITE

http://www.paramore.net

David Protess 1946-
American Educator, Legal Activist, and Journalist
Director of the Medill Innocence Project

BIRTH

David Protess was born on April 7, 1946, in the borough of Brooklyn in New York City. His father, Sidney Protess, was in business, and his mother, Beverly Gordon Protess, was a homemaker.

YOUTH

Growing up in the Sheepshead Bay neighborhood of Brooklyn, David Protess developed an early interest in social issues

———— " ————

Protess was deeply upset by the executions of convicted spies Julius and Ethel Rosenberg, especially by a newspaper headline that proclaimed "Rosenbergs Fried." "I can still recall standing there and seeing that," Protess remembered. "It seemed so unjust, and I'm not taking a position about whether they were guilty or not. What was unjust was that the state orphaned two young boys."

———— " ————

due to his mother's involvement in various causes. At age seven, an incident took place that focused his attention on one topic in particular. Julius and Ethel Rosenberg, a husband and wife, were convicted of spying for the Soviet Union and were sentenced to death. On June 19, 1953, they were put to death in the electric chair despite a worldwide campaign to stop their executions.

This highly publicized event had a lasting effect on Protess. He had been inspired by the efforts to spare the couple's lives, and his interest was heightened because he was the same age as one of the Rosenbergs' two sons. When the executions went ahead, Protess was deeply upset, and he grew angrier after reading a newspaper headline that proclaimed "Rosenbergs Fried." "I can still recall standing there and seeing that," he remembered. "It seemed so unjust, and I'm not taking a position about whether they were guilty or not. What was unjust was that the state orphaned two young boys." Decades later, Protess would return to the issues of crime and capital punishment—the execution of convicted criminals—which would become the center of his professional life.

EDUCATION

After graduating from high school, Protess moved to Chicago to attend Roosevelt University, where he earned a bachelor's degree in 1968. He went on to attend graduate school at the University of Chicago, earning a master's degree in 1970 and then a PhD (doctorate) in public policy in 1974 from the university's School of Social Service Administration.

CAREER HIGHLIGHTS

When his studies were completed, Protess took a job as a professor of political science at Loyola University in Chicago. He spent two years in that job, but he was also fascinated by another calling—investigative journalism. His interest was inspired by the Watergate scandal of the early 1970s. Watergate is the name of a hotel and office complex in Washington DC. In 1972, a group of people linked to President Richard M. Nixon were arrested while committing a burglary at the Watergate offices of the Democratic Party. After the failed burglary, Nixon and his aides created a massive cover-up to conceal any links between the burglars and the White House. But their efforts were unsuccessful. Over the course of the next two years, the involvement of the President and his aides in the burglary and the cover-up was revealed by many journalists and other investigators, but especially by two reporters at the *Washington Post,* Carl Bernstein and Bob Woodward. From that time on, the term "Watergate" became synonymous with the national scandal and the constitutional crisis that brought an end to Nixon's presidency and led to his decision to resign from office.

Protess was impressed by the work of the reporters who uncovered Watergate, and he realized that he wanted to devote himself to a similar type of work that would probe and publicize important issues. His wish came true in 1976, when he became the research director for the Better Government Association. An independent "watchdog" group based in Chicago, the association works to expose corruption and inefficiency in government. The job allowed Protess to demonstrate his skill in investigating the actions of public officials and employees. He also focused on writing newspaper stories during this period, and two articles that he authored for the *Chicago Sun Times* were named as finalists for the prestigious Pulitzer Prize.

As a journalist and in his investigative work for the Better Government Association, Protess carried on the tradition of the "muckrakers"—reporters who specialize in highlighting problems with the larger goal of changing public opinion and public policy on specific social issues. Muckraking writers had first become prominent during the progressive era of the late 1800s and early 1900s, and that style of crusading journalism enjoyed a resurgence beginning in the 1960s. "I just believe that the higher calling of journalism is that after you find the truth, you can in fact right the wrong," Protess explained.

A Professor with a Mission

In 1981, Protess once again took up the duties of a college professor, joining the faculty of the Medill School of Journalism at Northwestern University in Evanston, Illinois, near Chicago. Meanwhile, he continued to author investigative stories in his spare time, becoming a contributing editor and staff writer for *Chicago Lawyer* in 1986. In his work for that publication, Protess

Protess meeting with students while working on a case together in 1999.

specialized in sorting through the evidence in criminal cases and exposing instances where he believed there had been a miscarriage of justice.

By pursuing these stories, Protess was attempting to correct problems that he perceived within the criminal justice system. He noted that certain issues came up time and again in the cases he explored. In his opinion, police and prosecutors often made errors—sometimes by accident or carelessness and sometimes on purpose in order to attain a conviction. As a result, innocent people were jailed while the actual criminals went unpunished. In addition, he found that many defendants received poor legal representation, particularly those who had to rely on court-appointed lawyers because they could not afford to hire an attorney. These problems have been especially distressing for Protess when a wrongly convicted person has been sentenced to death. "No rational person would want to see an innocent person on death row or put to death," he noted. "And that's what's happening in … many cases."

Protess ultimately developed the idea of combining his teaching with his journalism projects. He began allowing students in his investigative reporting class to assist in his probes of questionable criminal cases, with their work counting toward their final grade in the course. This was a novel approach to teaching journalism, and it has proven to be very popular with students. At the beginning of each term, Protess presents the class with several cases in which there is a possibility that a person has been wrongly convicted. Students choose which case they want to explore and work in teams to pour through the facts.

Protess's students spend long hours reviewing court and police records, and they also "hit the street" to question people who may have knowledge about the crime, with the interviews frequently taking place in poor, inner-city neighborhoods in the Chicago area. Protess tries to prepare the class members for this difficult task by having them take part in role-playing exercises. In addition, a private investigator or Protess himself often accompanies the students on the real interviews, particularly those of crucial importance. While the work requires dedication and long hours, most members of the class become deeply devoted to their investigations. "You learn so much more from hands-on experience, talking to sources, digging for documents, getting information," explained Tom McCann, who took the class in the late 1990s. "That kind of investigative reporting fills you with so much adrenaline that you can't imagine doing anything else with your life."

"You learn so much more from hands-on experience, talking to sources, digging for documents, getting information," explained Tom McCann, one of Protess's students. "That kind of investigative reporting fills you with so much adrenaline that you can't imagine doing anything else with your life."

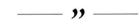

Success and Disappointment

One of the early cases that Protess and his students tackled involved the murder of a seven-year-old girl, Jaclyn Dowaliby, who went missing from her home in the Chicago suburb of Midlothian and was later found dead. Her parents, Cynthia and David Dowaliby, were accused of the crime. Charges were later dismissed against the mother, but in 1990, David Dowaliby was convicted of murder and sentenced to 45 years in prison. After covering the case for the *Chicago Tribune*, Protess continued to scrutinize the facts, calling on the assistance of his students and Rob Warden, the former publisher of *Chicago Lawyer*, who often collaborates with Protess.

Protess with the Ford Heights Four—(left to right) Willie Rainge, Kenny Adams, Dennis Williams, and Verneal Jimerson—who spent time in prison for a crime they didn't commit.

Because of the group's work, new evidence was discovered, and the main witness against Dowaliby recanted his court testimony. These developments helped to convince the Illinois Appellate Court to reverse the verdict, freeing David Dowaliby after more than a year in prison. In 1993, Protess and Warden published *Gone in the Night: The Dowaliby Family's Encounter with Murder and the Law*, which detailed their findings and their criticism of the official investigation and prosecution. It was the fifth book authored by Protess, who had previously written works on the subjects of social policy, citizen watchdog groups, and journalism. *Gone in the Night* was made into a made-for-TV movie that was broadcast in 1996.

While the Dowaliby case had been an encouraging experience for Protess, the project he and his students undertook in the early 1990s involving the case of Girvies Davis proved far less positive. In 1979, Davis had been convicted of murder and received the death sentence. Prosecutors had based their case on a written confession that Davis had given to police. But the suspect later maintained that officers had forced him to sign the document and had threatened to shoot him if he didn't admit that he was guilty of the crime. Moreover, Davis was illiterate, so it was impossible for him to read the confession he signed. Unfortunately for Davis, his court-appointed lawyer had never raised that important point during the trial.

After spending more than 15 years on death row, Davis was scheduled to be executed in 1995. Protess and his students spent six months attempting to get the authorities to reconsider the prisoner's guilt and to delay or cancel the execution, but in the early hours of May 17, 1995, Davis was put to death by lethal injection. Protess and the students who had worked on the project were devastated by the news, and a grief counselor was brought in to help them deal with the loss. While the prisoner's death was a heavy blow, it also provided Protess with a way forward. In the hours before he died, Davis had phoned Protess and his students, thanking them for their efforts on his behalf and asking them to assist a fellow prisoner on death row named Dennis Williams. Protess had agreed with the request, and when he convened his next investigative reporting class, students began looking into the facts surrounding the Williams conviction.

Four Innocent Men

On May 11, 1978, a young couple, Larry Lionberg and Carol Schmal, had been kidnapped during a gas station robbery in Homewood, Illinois. Their abductors took them to an abandoned house in the town of Ford Heights, where Schmal was raped and both she and Lionberg were shot to death. The brutal killings were front-page news, and several days later, four men were charged with the crime: Kenny Adams, Verneal Jimerson, Willie Rainge, and Dennis Williams. All four were black while the victims were white, adding a volatile racial element to the incident.

Police and prosecutors based their case largely on the testimony of Paula Gray, the girlfriend of Kenny Adams, who said she was present when the crime was committed. But Gray suffered from mental illness and an extremely low IQ, and her account of events changed dramatically over time. She initially said that the four had committed the crime, then recanted and said that police had forced her to implicate the men. Later, she once more reverted to her original story. Despite the inconsistency of Gray's statements, the accused men, who became known as the "Ford Heights Four," were found guilty and sent to prison. The questionable evidence and the shoddy work of defense lawyers led to numerous appeals, and the legal developments in the case stretched over many years. By the time that Protess and his investigative journalism class took up the case in January 1996, Adams and Rainge were still serving lengthy prison terms, and Williams was awaiting execution. Verneal Jimerson had gained his freedom in 1995, when the Illinois Supreme Court overturned his conviction.

Three college seniors in the class—Stephanie Goldstein, Stacey Delo, and Laura Sullivan—chose to investigate the charges against the Ford Heights

Four. In the months that followed, vital assistance was also supplied by René Brown, a private investigator who had worked on the case for a number of years, as well as several lawyers who agreed to contribute their services for no charge. By digging into the official files on the case, the students made an important discovery: the police had turned up evidence shortly after the murders took place that implicated four other men in the crime, but detectives had never followed up on the leads.

After an extensive amount of footwork, Protess, the students, and Brown were able to locate three of the four men who had been linked to the crime—one of whom was already in prison for another murder. In a stunning turn of events, two of the suspects confessed to the crime. Soon after, DNA testing confirmed that they had raped Carol Schmal and further proved that Williams, Adams, Rainge, and Jimerson were innocent. By July 1996, the charges against them had been officially dropped, and they were free men after an ordeal that marred 18 years of their lives. "We are victims of this crime, too," said Kenny Adams on the day that he was released from custody. "I want people to know that this could happen to anybody—and that's a crime."

> "We are victims of this crime, too," said exonerated prisoner Kenny Adams on the day that he was released from custody. "I want people to know that this could happen to anybody—and that's a crime."

In the Spotlight

The exoneration of the four men generated a tremendous number of media stories about the work of Protess and the students. The professor used the attention to emphasize his belief that police and prosecutors had knowingly ignored key evidence in the case in order to gain a quick conviction against the suspects they had initially arrested. "What we had here was a conspiracy to railroad four men," Protess said in *People*. "I've never seen anything this bad."

Some of the interest in the story had to do with the unusual circumstances of the investigation: young college students entering the dangerous streets of the inner city in order to win the freedom of innocent men. It sounded like the plot of a TV show or movie, so it was hardly surprising when the Walt Disney Company made a million-dollar offer for exclusive rights to the story, proposing to divide the money between the main participants, including Protess, the three students, and the Ford Heights Four. The deal ended up creating a rift between the professor and the students because

*Protess with Kenny Adams after his release from prison.
A member of the Ford Heights Four, Adams spent 18 years in prison before
Protess and his students proved he was innocent.*

Protess felt that all of the money should go to the former prisoners. "I do not intend to profit at the expense of these men," he stated. The students disagreed, and other players in the investigation, such as René Brown, were upset that they received little from the Disney offer. Ultimately, most of the money was divided five ways, with one share to the students and the rest to the former prisoners. In 1999, the wrongly convicted men won further compensation when they accepted a $36 million settlement in a civil suit they had filed against Cook County.

The book that addressed the case, *A Promise of Justice*, was authored by Protess and Rob Warden and was published in 1998 to mixed reviews. Some critics faulted the work for problems with the writing, including its unemotional, "just-the-facts" style, but *Booklist* found *A Promise of Justice* to be "an eloquent reminder of the justice system's flaws." The Disney film depiction of the Ford Heights case has yet to appear, but the work of Protess and his class members seems to have been the inspiration for a short-lived television series in the early 2000s. "Deadline" concerned a fictional college journalism professor who probes crimes with his students, but Protess had no involvement in the show. At one point, he even asked the producers of "Deadline" to confirm that fact publicly so that he wouldn't be mistakenly associated with the series.

A Last-Minute Cry for Help

Having gained a reputation for freeing the innocent, Protess was besieged with requests to help other prisoners. "My home number is scribbled on every death row in the country," he noted in *Newsweek*. In September 1998, a call came from an attorney who represented Anthony Porter, who was scheduled to be executed in Illinois just a few weeks later. Protess told the lawyer that he was unable to help because the prisoner would be put to death before his class could begin work on the case. Porter's chances looked dim, but just 48 hours before he was scheduled to die, he was granted a temporary stay of execution. The delay provided Protess's class with the time they needed, and a group of students began analyzing a crime that had occurred 16 years earlier.

"I'm not a critic of the legal system. I believe it works, and I think most people in prison are guilty," Protess explained. "But the more mail I received [about wrongly convicted prisoners], the more I began to question whether we had a serious problem on our hands."

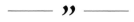

On a late summer evening in August of 1982, pistol shots rang out near a swimming pool in Washington Park in Chicago. The gunfire killed two teenagers, 18-year-old Jerry Hillard and his girlfriend, 19-year-old Marilyn Green. Two days later, Anthony Porter—a gang member who had previously been convicted of armed robbery—was charged with the crime. He was found guilty and assigned a cell on death row.

Prosecutors had relied heavily on a lead witness, William Taylor, who testified that he saw Porter shoot Hillard and Green. The students who took up the case began by checking Taylor's account of the crime. They staged a reenactment in the park, placing themselves in the positions that had been occupied by the victims, shooter, and the witness, and they realized that there was no way that the witness could have positively identified the killer in the nighttime darkness. "We couldn't make out our faces in the middle of the day," explained Shawn Armbrust, one of the class members probing the case. They also noted that the witness said that the killer fired the gun with his left hand, while Porter is right-handed.

These facts cast substantial doubt on the witness's account, so Protess and the students tracked down Taylor and interviewed him. He recanted his testimony, admitting that he had not seen the shooting. Instead, he said that police had "threatened, harassed, and intimidated" him until he

Former death row inmate Anthony Porter exuberantly hugs Protess after being released from prison due to the work of Protess and his students.

agreed to testify against Porter. Following another lead, the class members looked into the actions of two people who had been seen with Marilyn Green on the day of the murders—Alstory Simon and his wife at the time, Margaret Inez Jackson. Simon initially denied that he had anything to do with the killing, but when the students were finally able to find his ex-wife, she told a different story. The woman declared that Simon was the killer. Confronted with Jackson's videotaped statement, Simon confessed that he had shot Hillard and Green after he and Hillard had argued about money. On February 5, 1999, Anthony Porter walked out of prison after 16 years on death row and promptly hugged Protess and each of the students who had worked on his case.

Questioning Capital Punishment

The Porter case furthered Protess's reputation as a highly skilled investigator, but he has consistently downplayed his abilities as well as those of his students and other collaborators. Instead, he has stressed that his team's accomplishments are proof of the poor job that was done by police and prosecutors in the initial investigations. "It's not that we are so good," he argued. "Any kind of diligent effort in these cases could do what we did.… Which is what is so outrageous about a college professor and his students solving these crimes. They were there to be solved from the start."

Protess's success in achieving justice for wrongly convicted individuals has made him a focal point in the debate over alleged problems with the law enforcement and the courts. While he often denounces miscarriages of justice, Protess does not think the system is fundamentally flawed. "I'm not a critic of the legal system. I believe it works, and I think most people in prison are guilty," he explained. "But the more mail I received [about wrongly convicted prisoners], the more I began to question whether we had a serious problem on our hands."

Protess's views on capital punishment are much more firm. "I think that when it comes to the death penalty system in our country, the system is broken and can't be fixed." A primary complaint made by Protess and other critics is that many innocent people have been sentenced to death, and unless executions are ended, innocent people are going to be killed by the state. As proof of the problem, opponents of capital punishment cite the large number of individuals who have won their freedom while awaiting execution. According to the figures compiled by the Death Penalty Information Center, 139 death row inmates in the United States were exonerated of their crimes between 1973 and 2009. Commenting in 2004 on the national yearly averages of death row inmates winning their freedom, Protess noted that "for every seven people we put to death, one is exonerated. That error rate in a matter with life and death stakes is intolerably high."

The state of Illinois had a particularly poor record in this regard, with 13 inmates being released from death row between 1977 and 2000. The work of Protess and his students made a significant contribution to that number, and the publicity surrounding the Ford Heights and Anthony Porter cases helped focus public attention on the subject. In January 2000, Governor George Ryan responded to the situation by halting all executions in the state, and he directly mentioned the achievements of Protess's journalism class as a reason for his decision. Before leaving office in 2003, the governor went further, granting clemency to the 167 inmates then on death row, exempting them from ever being executed.

A Growing Movement

In 1999, Protess's investigative work with Northwestern students was organized under the name of the Medill Innocence Project, with the profes-

Protess leading a group of students in an Innocence Project meeting at Northwestern University, 2009.

sor serving as the institution's director. The new name reflected the fact that Protess and his colleagues were linked with similar groups around the country that seek to correct miscarriages of justice, many of which use the title "Innocence Project." Protess has been a leading figure in this movement, and in 2000, he became a founding member of the Innocence Network. This group includes journalism and law schools throughout the United States that are following the model established by Protess of involving students in the investigation of questionable legal proceedings.

In addition to correcting miscarriages of justice, Protess has turned his attention to helping freed prisoners adjust to life on the outside. In the early 2000s, he established a program to help the former inmates find employment and receive adequate health care and psychological treatment, naming it in memory of Dennis Williams of the Ford Heights Four, who died in 2003. This initiative got an important boost when Protess received the Puffin/Nation Prize for Creative Citizenship in 2003 and used part of the $100,000 prize money to fund the program.

Despite his other responsibilities, Protess continues to teach the investigative journalism course. As of 2009, the investigations carried out by the class have helped win the freedom of 11 innocent people, five of whom had been on death row. In addition, other investigations are in the works, one of which has been the subject of great media interest.

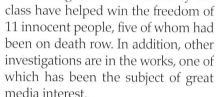

Protess's devotion to certain cases can become obsessive. "I go a little further than investigative reporters," he explained. "Once I feel I've reached a firm conclusion that someone is innocent, I can't think of something I wouldn't do to help them except break the law."

The case involves the conviction of Anthony McKinney for murdering a security guard in 1978 in the town of Harvey. It shares many of the elements that had figured in other Protess investigations. McKinney, who was 18 years old at the time of the crime, had signed a confession during questioning, but he later claimed that he did so only because he was beaten by police. An alleged eyewitness testified that he saw the teenager shoot the guard, but that witness later recanted his testimony and said that he, too, was brutalized by officers until he agreed to implicate McKinney. The investigation carried out by Protess's journalism students turned up other suspects, one of whom was in prison for a different murder. That man, Anthony Drake, admitted that he had been present when the security guard was shot and that McKinney was not involved in the crime.

Based on that information, a circuit court judge is considering a petition for a new trial for McKinney. But Cook County prosecutors are opposed to retrying the case, and they have tried to cast doubt on the work of Protess and his students. First, they subpoenaed grades, e-mail messages, and other information related to the students who investigated the case, in effect suggesting that the students' work is untrustworthy. A more sensa-

Flanked by the students whose records were subpoenaed, Protess speaks to reporters after a Cook County court hearing in Chicago, 2009.

tional development came in November 2009, when prosecutors accused the students of paying one of the witnesses in the case to provide a video statement to bolster McKinney's claims of innocence. Protess has strongly denied that charge. In addition, he has opposed the subpoena of information about his students, claiming that they were acting as journalists and deserve the protection of journalists' shield laws. These laws prevent law enforcement officials from requiring journalists to divulge their sources, since confidentiality is often crucial in getting sources to talk. Protess has suggested that Cook County prosecutors have ulterior motives for their approach. "Legally, what I take from it is that the prosecutors are on a fishing expedition," he said. "Practically, I think they have an interest in paying [us] back for years of embarrassment—and paying forward to deter us." The judge will conduct further hearings on the case in 2010.

A Controversial Crusader

Yet the McKinney case is not the first time that the work of Protess and his students has been scrutinized. A recurring charge against Protess is that he is more of an advocate for prisoners than a journalist. A journalist maintains his or her impartiality and detachment and tries to find the truth in an objective manner. But Protess, according to his critics, begins with the belief that convicts are innocent and tries to find evidence to support that belief. These critics have also argued that this bias could be reflected in the way the class is conducted, so that, for instance, students who uncover misdeeds by police or prosecutors receive higher grades than those who do not. Protess has maintained that he evaluates students on the quality of their work, regardless of their ultimate findings. Moreover, he has stressed that the majority of class investigations end up supporting the conviction. "In some cases, the truth was the guy was guilty, and those students [who made that determination] got an A."

Protess has admitted that he can become deeply involved in the subjects he investigates and that his devotion to certain cases can become obsessive. "I go a little further than investigative reporters," he explained. "Once I feel I've reached a firm conclusion that someone is innocent, I can't think of something I wouldn't do to help them except break the law." Not surprisingly, he has tried to instill a similar sense of commitment among the people who take his class. "I want to train students to think of their profession in broad terms," he said, "and not be afraid to shed their objectivity and get their hands dirty."

Though his job is demanding and often places him at the center of controversy, Protess has remained committed to his twin goals of freeing the innocent while also mentoring students who may go on to continue and expand that mission. "This is my life's work," he explained. "Sure, there are countless miscarriages of justice. I just hope I can be part of correcting them."

MARRIAGE AND FAMILY

Protess married Marianne Kreitman in 1969. The couple had one son, Daniel, and divorced in 1977. He wed Joan Perry in 1980 and has a second son, Benjamin, from that marriage.

WRITINGS

Community Power and Social Policy, 1974
Establishing a Citizens' Watchdog Group, 1979 (with Peter Manikas)
Uncovering Race: Press Coverage of Racial Issues in Chicago, 1989 (with James Ettema)
Agenda Setting: Readings on Media, Public Opinion, and Policymaking, 1991 (editor, with Maxwell McCombs)

Journalism of Outrage: Investigative Reporting and Agenda-Building in America, 1991 (with others)
Gone in the Night: The Dowaliby Family's Encounter with Murder and the Law, 1994 (with Robert Warden)
A Promise of Justice: The Eighteen-Year Fight to Save Four Innocent Men, 1998 (with Robert Warden)

HONORS AND AWARDS

National Teaching Award for Excellence in the Teaching of Journalism Ethics (Poynter Institute for Media Studies): 1986
Best Book of 1993 (Investigative Reporters and Editors): 1993, for *Gone in the Night*
Human Rights Award (National Alliance against Racist and Political Oppression): 1996
Person of the Week (ABC Network News): 1996
Champion of Justice Award (National Association of Criminal Defense Lawyers): 1997
Hal Lipset Truth in Action Award (World Association of Detectives): 1999
James McGuire Award (American Civil Liberties Union): 1999
H. Councill Trenholm Memorial Award (National Education Association): 2002
Clarence Darrow Award (Darrow Commemorative Committee): 2003
Herb Block Award (Newspaper Guild/Communication Workers of America): 2003
Puffin/Nation Prize for Creative Citizenship: 2003
Media Spotlight Award (Amnesty International)

FURTHER READING

Periodicals

American Journalism Review, June 1997, p.38
Biography, May 2000, p.100
Current Biography Yearbook, 1999
New York Times, Feb. 5, 1999, p.16; Mar. 6, 1999, p.7; Nov. 11, 2009, p.A20
Newsweek, May 31, 1999, p.32
People, July 29, 1996, p.44
Rolling Stone, Oct. 14, 1999, p.91

Online Articles

http://archives.chicagotribune.com/2009/oct/19/health/chi-nu-subpoena -19-oct19

(Chicago Tribune.com, "Northwestern University's Medill Innocence Project Is in a Standoff with Cook County Prosecutors," Oct. 19, 2009)
http://www.deathpenaltyinfo.org/innocence-list-those-freed-death-row
(Death Penalty Information Center, "The Innocence List," Nov. 3, 2009)
http://www.chron.org/tools/viewarticle.php?artid=677
(Northwestern Chronicle, "The Chronicle Interview: David Protess," Oct. 16, 2003)

ADDRESS

David Protess
Medill Innocence Project
1845 Sheridan Road
Evanston, IL 60208

WORLD WIDE WEB SITE

http://www.medillinnocenceproject.org

Albert Pujols 1980-

Dominican-Born American Professional Baseball
Player with the St. Louis Cardinals
National League Most Valuable Player in 2005, 2008,
and 2009

BIRTH

Jose Alberto Pujols (pronounced *POO-hoals*), known as Albert, was born on January 16, 1980, in Santo Domingo, Dominican Republic. The Dominican Republic is an island nation
located in the Caribbean Sea. Santo Domingo, its capital city,
lies on the southern coast.

Albert's mother left the family when he was three years old. His father, Bienvenido Pujols, was a painter who traveled frequently in search of work. As a result, Albert was raised primarily by his paternal grandmother, America Pujols, along with his father's 10 brothers and sisters. As an only child, Albert thought of his older aunts and uncles as siblings. He moved to the United States with his family in 1996, at the age of 16, and became an American citizen in 2007.

YOUTH

Albert grew up in a poor but close-knit family. During most of his childhood, he lived in run-down houses with dirt floors and no running water. His main interest was baseball, which he started playing at a young age. "I used to play catch with a lime," he remembered. "We made gloves out of cardboard milk boxes. Sticks were bats." He also watched American Major League Baseball (MLB) games on television whenever he had the chance and dreamed of playing professionally someday.

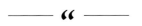

> *Growing up in the Dominican Republic, Pujol's main interest was baseball, which he started playing at a young age. "I used to play catch with a lime," he remembered. "We made gloves out of cardboard milk boxes. Sticks were bats."*

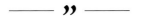

In the mid-1990s several members of the Pujols family decided to leave the Dominican Republic. They immigrated to the United States in hopes of building a better life for themselves. Albert and his father and grandmother joined them in 1996. After a brief stop in New York City, they settled in Independence, Missouri, where they joined a community of about 2,000 Dominican immigrants.

The Pujols family faced a difficult adjustment to life in the United States. They started out very poor, and it took a while for the older family members to find jobs. But Albert's grandmother made sure that he and the others were well cared for. "She gave me everything I needed," he recalled. "She supported me 100 percent. How they treated me and took care of me, that's where I learned everything." Albert's family even supported his dream of becoming a professional baseball player. "No one ever told me I couldn't be a big-league ballplayer," he noted. "They told me to keep working hard, that anyone who got there didn't get there easy."

EDUCATION

Pujols completed his early education in Santo Domingo. After moving to the United States in 1996, he entered Fort Osage High School in Independence as a sophomore. He spoke only Spanish at that time, so he struggled to fit in at school and keep up with his studies. He worked with a tutor, though, and learned to speak conversational English within a year. In spring 1997 Pujols tried out for the Fort Osage varsity baseball team. His incredible talent was obvious from the first time he took batting practice. "Every time he swung, the bat was just going crack, crack, crack," recalled his high school coach, Dave Fry. "I felt like the baseball gods had smiled down on me."

Pujols, shown here batting for the Prince William Cannons in 2000, played just one season in the minor leagues.

Pujols lived up to his early promise and had a remarkable high-school baseball career. He earned all-state honors as a sophomore with a .500 batting average and 11 home runs. During his junior year in 1998, he led Fort Osage to the Missouri state baseball championship and earned all-state honors for a second time. In only 33 at-bats, Pujols posted an outstanding .600 average and smacked 8 home runs as a junior—including a monster 450-footer that landed on top of a building located well beyond the fence of an opposing team's field. He actually came up to the plate a total of 88 times that season, but he also earned 55 walks (for statistical purposes, walks do not count as at-bats) because opposing teams were not willing to give him any good pitches to hit.

In January 1999, Pujols decided to forego his senior season of high school baseball and graduate early. Since opposing high school teams refused to pitch to him, he felt he could receive a better evaluation from professional baseball scouts by moving on to play college baseball. Pujols accepted a baseball scholarship to attend Maple Woods Community College in Kansas City. In his very first junior college game, he hit a grand slam and turned an unassisted triple play at shortstop.

Playing for Maple Woods, Pujols went on to bat .461 with 22 home runs and 80 runs batted in (RBIs). He left college that June, after completing only one semester, in order to pursue his dream of playing in the major leagues. Still, his single season of college baseball was quite memorable. "Coaches still talk about tape-measure shots Albert hit," recalled Maple Woods coach Marty Kilgore. "A ball he hit into somebody's backyard, over somebody's house, they're still fresh in the mind."

CAREER HIGHLIGHTS

Major League Baseball—The St. Louis Cardinals

Pujols had only played one season of college baseball, but he impressed professional baseball scouts enough to be selected in the 13th round of the 1999 MLB draft by the St. Louis Cardinals. He signed a contract for $10,000 and entered the Cardinals' minor league system in the spring of 2000. Pujols rocketed through the minor league ranks within a single season, turning in strong performances and earning repeated promotions to higher levels. During that one season, he played with the Class A Peoria Chiefs, the Class AA Potomac Cannons, and the Class AAA Memphis Redbirds. His accomplishments in the minor league system impressed the Cardinals' coaches, who invited him to join the big-league team for spring training in February 2001.

———— " ————

Pujols played four different positions during his rookie season—first base, third base, left field, and right field—but that didn't bother him. "I want to be in the lineup every day," he explained. "Playing anywhere is better than playing the bench."

———— " ————

When the Cardinals' coaching staff invited Pujols to attend spring training camp, they did not intend to give him a permanent slot on the roster. St. Louis had won the National League Central Division championship the year before, so the club did not desperately need young players. The coaches simply planned to give him a taste of the big leagues, then send him back to the minors to develop his skills for another year or two. As spring training progressed, however, Pujols played so well that the Cardinals had no choice but to keep him on the major league roster. "Each week when we had our cut meetings, there we were, figuring he had to go back to the minors at some point, and

*During his rookie season, shown here, Pujols batted .329 with
37 home runs and 130 RBIs.*

each week he kept impressing us more and more," recalled Cardinals General Manager Walt Jocketty. "It got to the final week and we just said, 'Look, we're really a better club with him,' the way he was playing."

Pujols first played in the major leagues on April 2, 2001, and he quickly became a vital member of the St. Louis lineup. His performance at the plate remained consistent even as the Cards struggled to find a defensive position for him. In fact, as his rookie season progressed, Pujols played in four different spots on the field—first base, third base, left field, and right field. But he claimed that shuffling around from infield to outfield did not bother him. "I want to be in the lineup every day," he explained. "Playing anywhere is better than playing the bench."

Pujols had one of the best rookie seasons in major league history. He batted .329 with 37 home runs, while walking 69 times and striking out only 93 times. He finished fifth in the National League in RBIs (with 130), hits (194), and doubles (47), and sixth in batting average and extra-base hits (88). His remarkable performance earned him National League Rookie of the Year honors. Pujols also provided the spark that helped the Cardinals successfully defend their Central Division championship with a 93-69 record, although St. Louis was defeated in the divisional playoff series by the Arizona Diamondbacks.

Pujols at first base in 2005, the year he won his first MVP award.

Working Hard to Prove Himself

Over the course of the 2002 season, Pujols established himself as one of the best young players in the league. He batted .314 with 34 home runs and 127 RBIs, while walking 72 times and reducing his strikeout total to 69. Thanks to his impressive performance, the young star finished second to Barry Bonds in the voting for the National League Most Valuable Player (MVP) award. Pujols's terrific season helped steer the Cardinals to a 97-65 record and their third straight National League Central Division crown. St.

Louis then swept the Diamondbacks in three straight games to advance to the National League Championship Series (NLCS). But the team fell short in its bid for a World Series appearance, losing to the San Francisco Giants in five games.

Throughout his first two seasons in the majors, Pujols demonstrated a remarkable combination of power, versatility, and consistency at the plate. He attributed his success as a hitter to his ability to recall pitchers' tendencies, recognize pitches, and make adjustments to his stance and swing as needed. "The main thing is I can read a pitcher. I can make adjustments," he noted. "That's how you become a good hitter, when you can tell yourself what you're doing wrong and correct it the next at-bat."

Even after making it to the majors, Pujols worked hard to develop his skills as a ball player. His preparation and desire to improve impressed his Cardinals teammates and coaches. He watched hours of videotape of different pitchers in order to study their movements. He also warmed up before each game by doing a long series of hitting drills, including some that were recommended to him by New York Yankees star Alex Rodriguez. Pujols's hard work and focus contributed to his success, and his natural ability was undoubtedly an important factor as well. "He's rare," said Cardinals' hitting coach Mitchell Page. "You look at that and you think of names like [Ted] Williams, [Rod] Carew, and [George] Brett, guys with beautiful, pure swings. Swings like his don't happen very often. It's a gift."

> *"The main thing is I can read a pitcher. I can make adjustments," Pujols noted. "That's how you become a good hitter, when you can tell yourself what you're doing wrong and correct it the next at-bat."*

Winning the National League Batting Title

Pujols played exceptionally well during his first two major league seasons—then set a new standard for himself in 2003. While the Cardinals fell short in their bid for a fourth consecutive divisional championship, St. Louis fans witnessed the emergence of a superstar. Pujols posted a league-leading .359 batting average to claim the National League batting title. He also led the league in runs scored (137), hits (212), and total bases (394). He added an impressive 43 home runs and 124 RBIs while also reducing his strikeout total to an amazing 65 in 591 at-bats. In honor of his achievements, Pujols was voted Player of the Year by his peers in the MLB Players Association. He fell short of claiming the National League MVP, however, finishing behind Bonds for the second straight year.

"He's rare," said Cardinals' hitting coach Mitchell Page. "You look at that and you think of names like [Ted] Williams, [Rod] Carew, and [George] Brett, guys with beautiful, pure swings. Swings like his don't happen very often. It's a gift."

In early 2004, the Cardinals signed Pujols to a seven-year, $100 million contract—making him the highest-paid player in team history. "His accomplishments in his first three seasons are unmatched in the history of the game," said team co-owner Bill DeWitt. "Albert Pujols will serve as a cornerstone for the Cardinals for many years to come." The Cardinals also announced that Pujols would play a single position in the field for the first time in his major league career: first base. His coaches felt that this defensive position, which is considered less physically demanding than most others, would reduce his chance of injury and allow him to focus on his hitting.

As the 2004 season got underway, Pujols started out slowly. He struggled with chronic injuries to his heel and elbow for much of the year. As a result, he endured the first hitting slump of his career, which caused his batting average to dip below .300 at the end of May. But then his wife—an avid softball player—watched some videotapes of his swing and suggested that he narrow his batting stance. Pujols made the adjustment and immediately went on an offensive tear, hitting six home runs in the next nine games.

Pujols ended the 2004 season batting .331 with 46 home runs and 123 RBIs. St. Louis won an impressive 105 games to return to the top of the National League Central Division. The Cardinals swept the Los Angeles Dodgers in the divisional series, then defeated the Houston Astros in a tough seven-game NLCS to reach the World Series. Pujols was named the NLCS MVP, with a .500 batting average, 5 home runs, and 11 RBIs. Unfortunately for Pujols and his teammates, however, the promising season ended in disappointing fashion. The Cardinals lost the World Series to the Boston Red Sox in a four-game sweep. "It was great to be there," Pujols noted, "but it's too bad the way we played. You look at our season and you think, 'There's no way these guys are going to get swept.' But that's how this game is. We just have to forget about what happened and get ready for this year."

Claiming a World Series Championship

During the 2005 season Pujols turned in one of the best performances of his young career, batting .330 with 41 home runs and 117 RBIs. With rival Barry Bonds sidelined for most of the season with a knee injury, Pujols finally claimed his first National League MVP Award. Although he was pleased to receive the prestigious award, he insisted that the team's success was more important than individual honors. "I don't think about that stuff," he said. "I don't worry about winning the MVP, the batting title, or home runs. I just want to help my team out. If I do that, my numbers are going to be there."

Pujols and his teammates dominated their division in 2005 and finished the year with the best record in baseball at 100-62. With Pujols batting .556 in the playoffs, the heavily favored Cardinals swept the San Diego Padres in the National League Division Series. But the Cards fell short in their bid for a return trip to the World Series. Despite a dramatic game-winning homer by Pujols in Game 5, St. Louis was eliminated in the NLCS by the Houston Astros.

As the 2006 season got underway, Pujols was determined to achieve his dream of winning a World Series title. He got off to the hottest start in the history of baseball, hitting 19 home runs in the first 38 games of the season. He even tied an MLB record by hitting home runs in four consecutive at-bats. Yet he still insisted that he did not consider himself to be a home-run hitter. "[Mark] McGwire's a home run hitter, Bonds is a home run hitter," he explained. "I'm a line-drive hitter with power, and that's it. All I try to do is just hit for average, and hopefully if I put a good swing on it the ball's going to go out of the park."

Although he was nagged by injuries later in the 2006 season, Pujols still managed to post a career-high 49 home runs and 137 RBIs to go with his .331 batting average. After squeaking out a division title with 83 victories, the Cardinals defeated the San Diego Padres in the divisional playoff series. Then St. Louis survived a dramatic, seven-game NLCS against the New York Mets to earn a trip back to the World Series, facing the Detroit Tigers.

Pujols did not play his best during the series, batting only .200 with one homer. Still, the Cardinals managed to defeat the Tigers in five games to claim the World Series championship. "Now I can say I have a World Series ring in my trophy case," Pujols said afterward. "And that's what you play for. It doesn't matter how much money you make or what kind of numbers you put up in the big leagues. If you walk out of this game and you don't have a ring, you haven't accomplished everything." Although he

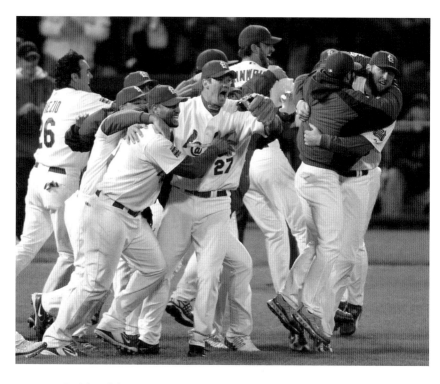

Pujols celebrating with teammates after the St. Louis Cardinals defeated the Detroit Tigers to win the 2006 World Series.

was disappointed to finish second to Ryan Howard in the 2006 National League MVP race, Pujols was delighted to be honored for his defensive play by winning his first Rawlings Gold Glove Award.

Earning Back-to-Back MVP Awards

The Cardinals followed up their World Series title with a disappointing season in 2007. Pujols struggled with a torn ligament and bone spurs in his right elbow for much of the year. He still managed to hit .327 with 32 home runs and 103 RBIs, but the Cardinals finished six games below .500 and failed to make the playoffs. But Pujols accomplished an important personal triumph during the offseason: he scored 100 percent on his citizenship test and officially became a U.S. citizen.

The Cardinals continued to struggle in 2008, winning only 86 games to finish 11 1/2 games out of first place in the division. But Pujols overcame his elbow problems to post one of the greatest individual seasons in baseball history. After starting the season with a 42-game hitting streak, he finished second in the race for the batting title with a .357 average, while adding 37 home runs and 116 RBIs. Pujols was named Player of the Year by the MLB Players Association and also claimed the second National League MVP Award of his career. "I have to thank my teammates," he said afterward. "Obviously this is not an award that you win by yourself. My teammates were involved every day, day in and day out, supporting me, getting on base and driving me in. These kind of numbers, you can't do it by yourself." Following the 2008 season, Pujols had surgery to repair nerve damage in his elbow.

After the surgery, Pujols returned to top form in 2009. He batted .330 with 47 home runs and 134 RBIs to soar to his second straight MVP Award—and the third of his illustrious career. His strong performance helped St. Louis become the first to clinch the top spot in its division. Pujols and his teammates entered the 2009 playoffs with high hopes, only to see them dashed in the first round. The Cardinals failed to win a single playoff game, losing the divisional series to the Los Angeles Dodgers in three games. "I don't like the stigma of our club getting swept," St. Louis manager Tony LaRussa said afterward. "We're a better club than that, and the series was more competitive than that. But that's what it is."

"Now I can say I have a World Series ring in my trophy case," Pujols said. "And that's what you play for. It doesn't matter how much money you make or what kind of numbers you put up in the big leagues. If you walk out of this game and you don't have a ring, you haven't accomplished everything."

Emerging as the Best Hitter in Baseball

By the time he received his third career MVP trophy, Pujols was widely considered to be among the best hitters in baseball history. His career batting average of .334 ranked the highest among all active players, and he also contributed a total of 366 home runs and 1,112 RBIs. He was the first player ever to hit .300 or better with at least 30 home runs and 100 RBI in each of his first nine MLB seasons. "If you define an effective hitter simply in terms of the runs he produces, Pujols is just the best in the game—a tremendous power hitter who seldom strikes out," baseball analyst Caleb Peiffer declared. "He might be the best right-handed hitter in baseball history." At the conclusion of the 2009 season, *Sporting News* named Pujols as

Pujols is widely considered one of the best hitters in the history of baseball.

Major League Baseball's Athlete of the Decade. Among St. Louis fans, he is known simply as El Hombre, which means "the man" in Spanish.

Perhaps the most remarkable thing about Pujols is that, by all accounts, he has achieved his success by working hard rather than by cheating. Unlike many other big hitters, he has never tested positive for performance-enhancing drugs or been implicated in any investigations of illegal steroid use. "After a decade of dirtiness and suspicion regarding some of the game's premier sluggers using steroids or being accused of such indiscretion," wrote Jon Saraceno in *USA Today,* "Pujols makes fans feel good again." In fact, Pujols has offered to undergo frequent, voluntary drug testing and promised to return every penny of his salary if the results are ever positive. "He isn't colorful and he isn't controversial," said LaRussa. "He's just great."

Among the Cardinals' top priorities for the 2010 season is to sign Pujols to another long-term contract. His existing deal is scheduled to end following the 2011 season, and he almost certainly stands to earn more money by changing teams. When asked about the contract situation in interviews, he indicated that he wants to remain in St. Louis, but only if Cardinals management continues to demonstrate a commitment to building a winning team. "It's not about the money all the time," he stated. "It's about being in a place to win and being in a position to win."

Despite all the praise and awards he has received, Pujols has remained humble and continued to work hard to improve his game. "He works harder than any hitter I've ever seen and studies the tendencies pitchers use to work him," said teammate Ryan Ludwick. "It's rare for a pitcher to get him out the same way. He adjusts so well, rarely gets fooled, and is never outmatched." Pujols has said that hard work and dedication are the secrets to his long-term success. "One of the mistakes a lot of young players make is that once they get to the big leagues, they think, 'That's it,' and they don't work that hard," he explained. "But you have to work extra hard to get better. The older you get, the more you have to work to get better. I'm still working hard every day."

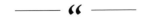

Pujols has said that hard work and dedication are the secrets to his long-term success. "One of the mistakes a lot of young players make is that once they get to the big leagues, they think, 'That's it,' and they don't work that hard," he explained. "But you have to work extra hard to get better. The older you get, the more you have to work to get better. I'm still working hard every day."

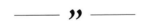

MARRIAGE AND FAMILY

Pujols met his wife, Deidre Corona (known as Dee Dee), at a Latin dance club in Kansas City. He was 18 and still in high school at the time, while she was 21 and a college graduate. She had recently given birth to a daughter, Isabella, with Down Syndrome (a genetic disorder that occurs in one of every 800 births and results in various physical problems and moderate mental retardation). Despite the difference in their ages and situations, the couple began dating and soon fell in love.

Pujols married Dee Dee on New Year's Day in 2000, and he adopted Isabella a short time later. They had a son, Alberto Jose (known as A.J.), in January 2001, shortly before Pujols's stellar rookie year with the Cardinals. They added another daughter, Sophia, to their family in November 2005, around the time Albert won his first MVP. The Pujols live in the comfortable St. Louis suburb of Creve Coeur. Pujols takes every available opportunity to emphasize the importance of family in his life. "Dee Dee is the best wife. She's my cheerleader," he stated. "My kids are the best thing that ever happened to me. God and my family are why I do everything."

HOBBIES AND OTHER INTERESTS

Pujols says that he does not have time for hobbies. "I spend time with my family," he noted. "That's my hobby. That's it. Family and baseball." But he ranks among the most generous MLB players when it comes to charity work. He and his wife founded the Pujols Family Foundation in 2005 to help people with Down Syndrome and to support impoverished families in the Dominican Republic. In 2009 the foundation donated $70,000 to St. Luke's Hospital in St. Louis to open a wellness center for adults with Down Syndrome. Pujols also took a team of volunteer doctors and dentists to the Dominican Republic to provide health care to poor children.

Pujols received the prestigious Roberto Clemente Award in 2009 as the MLB player who best combined excellence on the field with service to the community. "I don't want to be remembered as the best baseball player ever," he stated. "I want to be remembered as a great guy who loved the Lord, loved to serve the community, and who gave back. That's the guy I want to be remembered as when I'm done wearing this uniform. That's from the bottom of my heart."

AWARDS AND HONORS

National League Rookie of the Year (Baseball Writers' Association of America): 2001

National League All-Star Team: 2001, 2003-2009

National League Batting Champion: 2003

National League Player of the Year (MLB Players Association): 2003, 2008, 2009

National League Most Valuable Player: 2005, 2008, 2009
World Series championship: 2006, with St. Louis Cardinals
Gold Glove Award: 2006
Roberto Clemente Award: 2008
Major League Baseball Athlete of the Decade (*Sporting News*): 2009

FURTHER READING

Books

Abrams, Dennis. *Baseball Superstars: Albert Pujols,* 2008 (juvenile)
Christopher, Matt. *On the Field with ... Albert Pujols,* 2009 (juvenile)
Needham, Tom. *Albert Pujols: MVP on and off the Field,* 2009 (juvenile)
Rains, Rob. *Albert Pujols: Simply the Best,* 2009 (juvenile)

Periodicals

Baseball Digest, Dec. 2001, p.46; Nov. 2002, p.48; Oct. 2003, p.22; Feb. 2004,
    p.38; Aug. 2005, p.50; Jan.-Feb. 2009, p.38
Current Biography Yearbook, 2004
Kansas City (MO) Star, Oct. 9, 2001, p.C1; June 27, 2004, p.C1
New York Times, Nov. 18, 2008, p.B18
St. Louis Post-Dispatch, May 20, 2001, p.D1; Mar. 30, 2003, p.4; Feb. 21,
    2004, p.3
Sports Illustrated, Apr. 16, 2001, p.48; Oct. 1, 2001, p.44; June 30, 2003, p.32;
    May 22, 2006, p.58; Nov. 8, 2006, p.48; Mar. 16, 2009, p.28
USA Today, May 22, 2001, p.C1; May 15, 2006, p.C6; May 23, 2006, p.C1;
    Mar. 31, 2009, p.C1; July 13, 2009, p.C1

ADDRESS

Albert Pujols
St. Louis Cardinals
250 Stadium Plaza
St. Louis, MO 63102

WORLD WIDE WEB SITES

http://stlouis.cardinals.mlb.com
http://www.pujolsfamilyfoundation.org

Sonia Sotomayor 1954-

American Supreme Court Justice
First Hispanic Justice on the U.S. Supreme Court

BIRTH

Sonia Sotomayor (pronounced *so-toe-my-OR*) was born on June 23, 1954, in the Bronx, the northernmost of the five boroughs that make up New York City. She was the daughter of Puerto Rican immigrants who came to the United States during World War II. Her father, Juan, had only a third-grade education and never learned to speak English. He worked as a welder after arriving in the United States. Her mother, Celina,

Sotomayor at the age of six or seven.

first worked as a telephone operator at a small hospital in the Bronx. She later earned her practical nurse's license and worked as a methadone clinic nurse and emergency room supervisor. Sonia has one younger brother, Juan, who grew up to become a doctor.

YOUTH

Sotomayor was born and raised in a housing project in the Bronx, a rough, working-class part of New York that experienced rising rates of crime and poverty during her childhood and adolescence. Fortunately, the Sotomayor family was able to obtain an apartment in the Bronxdale Houses, a complex that was much cleaner and safer than some of the other housing options in the Bronx. Unlike the graffiti- and trash-strewn housing that marred other parts of the Bronx, these residential apartments were, as Sonia recalled, "spacious and pristine."

The challenges of growing up in the Bronx became even greater for Sotomayor in 1962, when she was diagnosed with diabetes at age eight. Diabetes is a disease in which the pancreas is no longer able to produce insulin, a hormone that enables the body to process sugars in food. If left untreated, it can cause blindness, heart disease, and kidney problems. Sotomayor's family, however, was able to bring her diabetes under control through careful monitoring and daily injections of insulin. Today, Sotomayor continues to give herself daily insulin injections to manage her diabetes.

One year after Sotomayor was diagnosed with diabetes, her father suffered a fatal heart attack at the young age of 42. This sudden loss devastated the family and forced Celina Sotomayor to support and raise her children all by herself. She worked extra hours to put her children through private Catholic schools, and she even scrimped and saved to buy Sonia and her brother a full *Encyclopaedia Britannica* set. According to her children, their encyclopedia set was the only one in the entire housing project.

Celina Sotomayor also set firm guidelines of behavior for her children. "They had their rules," recalled one of Sonia's childhood friends. "She worked, and basically no one was allowed out of the house until she came home from work." In addition, she was a steady role model who taught her children the importance of education and the value of hard work. When Sonia was a teenager, for example, her mother returned to school to become a registered nurse. "My mom was like no student I knew," Sonia recalled. "She got home from school or work and literally immersed herself in her studies, working until midnight or beyond, only to get up again before all of us.… She had almost a fanatical emphasis on education.… She kept saying, 'I don't care what you do, but be the best at it.'"

An Early Passion for Justice

Young Sotomayor took her mother's lessons to heart. She became known in her neighborhood as both a spunky and principled kid. Her younger brother recalls that she frequently stepped in to defend him from local bullies. She also developed an early fascination with the adventures of popular crime-fighting heroes of the 1950s and 1960s. Her two favorites were Nancy Drew, a high-spirited girl detective featured in a series of children's books, and Perry Mason, a brilliant and idealistic lawyer who solved mysteries on a television series that broadcast from 1957 to 1966. "When I was nine or ten, I became enamored of Nancy Drew stories and I wanted to be an investigative detective like her," Sotomayor noted. When doctors told Sonia that her diabetes would prevent her from pursuing detective work, she was crestfallen. But her disappointment was short-lived. "I noticed that Perry Mason was involved in a lot of the same kinds of investigative work that I had been fascinated with reading Nancy Drew, so I decided to become a lawyer," she explained. "Once I focused on becoming a lawyer, I never deviated from that goal."

Celina Sotomayor was a strong role model who valued education and hard work. She set firm guidelines of behavior for her children. "They had their rules," recalled one of Sonia's childhood friends. "She worked, and basically no one was allowed out of the house until she came home from work."

EDUCATION

Sotomayor attended Catholic private schools in the Bronx throughout her elementary and high school years. An excellent and hardworking student,

Sotomayor as a Princeton senior when she won the Pyne Prize, the highest academic honor granted to an undergraduate student.

she was class valedictorian when she graduated from Cardinal Spellman High School in 1972.

Sotomayor's fine academic record enabled her to gain admission into New Jersey's Princeton University, one of eight famous "Ivy League" colleges in the northeastern United States. Upon arriving on Princeton's campus in the fall of 1972, however, Sotomayor recalled that the school constituted "a very foreign experience for someone from the South Bronx." For one thing, Princeton had only begun admitting women a few years before, so most of the student body was male. In addition, she had grown up surrounded by Latino friends, classmates, and neighbors, but there were few other Latinos in Princeton's student body—and none on its faculty.

The sense of isolation and uncertainty that Sotomayor initially felt at Princeton grew worse when she realized that she did not possess the same level of background knowledge as her classmates, most of whom came from wealthy families and fancy prep schools. Determined to close this gap, Sotomayor devoted much of her freshman year to reading the works of Mark Twain, Jane Austen, and other famous writers taught in prep school literature courses. "She was very studious and intent on doing well in school," one of her friends recalled. "I remember her emerging sometimes in the early morning from her room, somewhat rumpled. I knew she spent all night working on a paper or studying.… If she had a project to do, she worked on it 100 percent."

Sotomayor soon overcame these initial struggles with her grit and determination. By her junior year she was not only posting top grades, but was also emerging as a leader of campus Latino groups. She earned top academic marks as a senior as well, enabling her to graduate summa cum laude ("with highest praise") with a bachelor's degree in history in 1976. In fact, Sotomayor was honored as a senior with the Pyne Prize, the school's highest academic honor for undergraduate students. This recognition marked the first time that Princeton had awarded the Pyne Prize to a Latino student.

Years later, Sotomayor described her four years at Princeton as "the single most transforming experience" of her life. Speaking at Princeton in 1996 to a group of Latino students, she explained that "it was here that I became truly aware of my Latina identity—something I had taken for granted during my childhood when I was surrounded by my family and their friends."

Armed with her degree from Princeton, Sotomayor decided to pursue a law degree at Yale, another famous Ivy League school bursting with wealthy and privileged students. Like she had done at Princeton, Sotomayor displayed both ambition and talent during her years at the Yale Law School. By the time she graduated in 1979, she had served a stint as editor of the prestigious *Yale Law Journal,* co-chaired the Latin American and Native American Students Association, and worked as managing editor of the Yale Studies in World Public Order program. "She had such a different path," recalled one of her law school friends. "There were so many people [at Yale] that had Roman numerals after their names and long histories of family members who had gone to Yale, and here was this woman who was from the projects, not hiding her views at all, just totally outspoken. She's one of those where, even at a school with great people, I knew that she was going to go on and do amazing things."

"She was very studious and intent on doing well in school," one of Sotomayor's *college friends recalled. "I remember her emerging sometimes in the early morning from her room, somewhat rumpled. I knew she spent all night working on a paper or studying.... If she had a project to do, she worked on it 100 percent."*

FIRST JOBS

After earning her law degree, Sotomayor left the leafy Yale campus for a position in New York City's office of the district attorney (DA). In a criminal case, the DA works as the prosecutor, the lawyer who represent the government in charging someone with a crime, while the defense attorney is the lawyer who represents the accused person. As an assistant DA, Sotomayor represented the city in numerous criminal cases involving robbery, assault, murder, rape, police brutality, prostitution, and other crimes.

"My work ran the gamut of criminal activity," she later said. "It was wonderful training for a lawyer."

Sotomayor admitted, however, that her work obtaining criminal convictions against alleged wrongdoers was sometimes difficult. "I had more problems during my first year in the office with the low-grade crimes—the shoplifting, the prostitution, the minor assault cases," she explained. "In large measure, in those cases you were dealing with … crimes that could be the product of the environment and of poverty. Once I started doing felonies, it became less hard. No matter how liberal I am, I'm still outraged by crimes of violence. Regardless of whether I can sympathize with the causes that lead these individuals to do these crimes, the effects are outrageous."

Sotomayor also acknowledged that some cases lingered longer than others. "It pains me," she said, "when I meet particularly bright defendants—and I've met quite a few of them—people who, if they had had the right guidance, the right education, the right breaks, could have been contributing members of our society. When they get convicted, there's a satisfaction, because they're doing things that are dangerous. But there are also nights when I sit back and say, 'My God, what a waste!'"

In 1984 Sotomayor left the DA's office for a job with the private New York law firm of Pavia and Harcourt. For the next several years she worked primarily on intellectual property issues and international commercial law. In 1988 she was promoted to partner in the firm.

CAREER HIGHLIGHTS

Launching a Career as a Judge

Sotomayor left private law practice and launched her career as a judge in 1991. That year, Republican President George H.W. Bush, acting on the recommendation of New York Democratic Senator Daniel Patrick Moynihan, nominated her to become a federal district judge in the Southern District of the State of New York. Sotomayor was honored by the nomination and happily accepted. When her nomination was confirmed in August 1992, she became the first American of Hispanic descent to be appointed to the federal bench in New York.

Sotomayor spent six years as a district judge. During this period she became known as a decisive, no-nonsense judge who had little patience for unprepared lawyers, political schemers, or legal games. Her most celebrated case during her tenure as a district judge came in April 1995, when she delivered a momentous ruling on a bitter eight-month-long legal battle between Major League Baseball owners and players over salary issues. This conflict

THE U.S. JUDICIAL SYSTEM

The court system, or judicial system, is one of the three branches of the federal government set out in the U.S. Constitution: the executive branch, the legislative branch, and the judicial branch. Each branch has specific responsibilities. The executive branch includes the president and the vice president. It also includes the Cabinet, a group of presidential advisers who are the heads of federal departments and agencies, including the departments of state, treasury, defense, justice, education, and others. The legislative branch is the Congress, including both the House of Representatives and the Senate. The Congress creates laws, collects taxes, declares war, ratifies treaties, and approves the president's nominations for certain positions, including federal judges. The judicial branch includes the nation's courts.

The federal judicial system, where Sotomayor served, is comprised of three different levels. The lower courts, the level at which most cases are originally tried (and where Sotomayor started her career as a judge), are the district courts. After a case is tried, if one side disagrees with the decision of the district court and wants to appeal it, the case would go to the next level, the court of appeals. There are 94 judicial districts in the U.S., and those districts are organized into 12 regional circuits, each of which maintains a U.S. Court of Appeals (also called circuit courts). The appeals (or appellate) court judges review the lower court's decision and either sustain it (agree) or overturn it (disagree). After that step, the case could be taken to the Supreme Court, the highest court in the land. The decision of the Supreme Court is final. At all three levels in the U.S. judicial system, federal judges are nominated by the president, confirmed by the Senate, and serve for life.

had arisen when team owners tried to sweep away longstanding free agent and salary arbitration systems. The players, who strongly supported these systems, had responded to this move by going out on strike. The conflict was so entrenched that the 1994 World Series had to be cancelled.

Sotomayor settled this clash by issuing an injunction (essentially a court order) against the team owners. She ruled that the owners had no legal right to unilaterally end Major League Baseball's free agent and salary arbitration systems. That ruling forced the owners to return to the bargaining table. A short time later, players and owners reached a new agreement that ended the longest work stoppage in professional sports history.

Moving to the Court of Appeals

In 1997 President Bill Clinton nominated Sotomayor to become a judge on the U.S. Court of Appeals for the Second Circuit. Judges on these appeals courts review legal decisions handed down by district courts, as well as those handed down by federal agencies. Cases heard in appeals courts are reviewed by three-judge panels, which have the power to reverse these decisions if a majority of the three judges feel that the lower court or agency has issued an unconstitutional or otherwise flawed decision.

———— **"** ————

"The practice of law is perhaps the most diverse, eclectic exposure to life that you can receive," Sotomayor explained. *"People come to you with their problems, and their cases cover a wide range of issues. For you to be able to practice law with the vision it requires, you have to be a very well-rounded person because whatever happens out in the real world, whether it involves business or family or technology, usually finds its way into the courtroom."*

———— **"** ————

Sotomayor's nomination to the Court of Appeals was confirmed by the U.S. Senate on October 2, 1998. She loved working as an appeals court judge, in large measure because she enjoyed the intellectual challenge of hearing all sorts of different cases involving numerous complex legal issues. "The practice of law is perhaps the most diverse, eclectic exposure to life that you can receive," she explained. "People come to you with their problems, and their cases cover a wide range of issues. For you to be able to practice law with the vision it requires, you have to be a very well-rounded person because whatever happens out in the real world, whether it involves business or family or technology, usually finds its way into the courtroom."

Sotomayor's position on the Second Circuit also enabled her to keep living in her beloved New York City. Working from her home base—a stylish two-bedroom condominium in the city's vibrant Greenwich Village neighborhood—she loved to explore the city's many restaurant, theatre, sports, and nightlife options. She sometimes embarked on these adventures with current and former law clerks from her staff, many of whom she regarded as members of her extended family.

Sotomayor poses by her office window in 1998, after being confirmed by the U.S. Senate for a seat on the U.S. Court of Appeals for the Second Circuit.

On the bench, meanwhile, Sotomayor's reputation continued to grow. Lawyers who appeared before her court regarded her as smart and fair-minded, but they also knew that she could be tough on lawyers who were not ready for court. As one former Sotomayor clerk-turned-U.S. attorney stated, "[she] doesn't tolerate unpreparedness, nor should she."

During the course of her career on the appeals court, Sotomayor heard appeals of more than 3,000 cases and wrote about 380 majority opinions. The U.S. Supreme Court reviewed a total of five of these cases. It reversed the majority decision supported by Sotomayor on three occasions. The most highly publicized of these reversals came in June 2009, when the Supreme Court ruled by a narrow 5-4 margin that Sotomayor erred in supporting a decision by the city of New Haven, Connecticut, to toss out a promotion test used by the fire department. The Supreme Court majority ruled that white firefighters who had scored well on the test were unfairly denied promotions when the results were thrown out.

Nominated for the Highest Court in the Land

Sotomayor's life took a momentous turn in November 2008, when Democrat Barack Obama defeated Republican candidate John McCain in the presidential election to become the nation's 44th president. Sotomayor knew that Obama's victory might have enormous consequences for her. Political and legal analysts alike agreed that if Obama had an opportunity to fill an opening on the U.S. Supreme Court during his presidency, Sotomayor ranked as one of the top candidates. They believed that he would be attracted by her strong legal qualifications, her inspiring life story, and the prospect of nominating the first Latino American to the nation's highest court.

Sotomayor listened to this speculation with mixed feelings. She knew that a seat on the U.S. Supreme Court was the pinnacle of her profession. The nine justices who sit on the Supreme Court may hold office for life. The Supreme Court's job is to make sure laws passed by the legislative branch and regulations issued by the executive branch do not violate the U.S. Constitution, which is the cornerstone of all American law. The Court accomplishes this by interpreting the provisions of the Constitution and applying its rules to specific legal cases. Because the Constitution lays out general rules, the Court tries to determine their meaning and figure out how to apply them to modern situations. After the justices select a case for review—and they accept fewer than about 100 of the 6,000 cases presented to them each year—they first will hear arguments by the two opposing sides. They begin discussing the case, take a preliminary vote, and then

President Barack Obama and Vice President Joe Biden escort Sotomayor to the East Room of the White House, where the president introduced her as his nominee for the U.S. Supreme Court, May 2009.

one justice from the majority is assigned to write up the Court's opinion. Drafting an opinion is complex and time-consuming, and the whole process can take over a year. The Court's final opinion has tremendous importance, setting out a precedent that all lower courts and all levels of government throughout the United States are required to follow. The reasoning given in the opinion is also important, because it helps people understand the basis for the decision and how the ruling might apply to other cases in the future.

Despite the power and prestige associated with becoming a Supreme Court judge, Sotomayor was not sure that she wanted to rebuild a new life for herself in Washington DC, where the Supreme Court hears cases. "Sonia was happy being a Federal Appeals judge, loved her life in New York, and felt fulfilled," a friend noted. "She worried about having less time to spend with her mother, family, and friends, particularly given her mom's age and potential health complications."

In the end, though, Sotomayor decided that she would accept a nomination if it was offered. She knew that as the country's first Latino Supreme Court justice—and only the third woman justice in the long history of the

Court—she could be a role model and inspiration to millions of minority children across the country.

On May 1, 2009, Supreme Court Justice David H. Souter announced that he intended to retire. White House officials quickly contacted Sotomayor and a few other leading candidates to interview them for the Supreme Court opening. During the next few weeks, officials combed through the personal histories and legal decisions of the candidates, who also sat for long rounds of interviews with members of Obama's staff. Then, on the evening of May 25, Sotomayor received a telephone call from the White House saying that the president would like to speak to her. "I had my cell phone in my right hand and I had my left hand over my chest trying to calm my beating heart, literally," she remembered. "And the president got on the phone and said to me, 'Judge, I would like to announce you as my selection to be the next Associate Justice of the United States Supreme Court.' I caught my breath and started to cry and said, 'Thank you, Mr. President.'"

> **"I had my cell phone in my right hand and I had my left hand over my chest trying to calm my beating heart, literally," Sotomayor remembered. "And the president got on the phone and said to me, 'Judge, I would like to announce you as my selection to be the next Associate Justice of the United States Supreme Court.' I caught my breath and started to cry and said, 'Thank you, Mr. President.'"**

Before concluding their phone conversation, Obama asked her for two promises. "The first was to remain the person I was, and the second was to stay connected to my community," she said. "And I said to him that those were two easy promises to make, because those two things I could not change."

Enduring a Challenging Confirmation Process

When Obama announced that he intended to send Sotomayor's nomination to the U.S. Senate for confirmation, as required by law, he emphasized both her amazing personal story and her distinguished judicial career. The president also discussed "empathy"—the ability to understand and identify with another person's feelings and views. He said that Sotomayor possessed the empathy he was looking for in a Supreme Court justice.

Many observers warmly praised Obama's pick. Leaders from America's Latino communities expressed delight with the selection, as did progressive political activists, Democratic lawmakers, and many legal scholars. Republican congressional leaders and conservative pundits strongly criticized the choice, however. They charged, for instance, that "empathy" was simply a code word to describe a judge who favored changing laws to fit his or her liberal political beliefs. They pressed these claims even after Sotomayor supporters noted that Supreme Court Justice Samuel Alito—a conservative whose nomination a few years earlier had been embraced by Republicans—had trumpeted the value of empathy in his own Supreme Court confirmation hearings.

Conservative opponents of Sotomayor's nomination also highlighted the U.S. Supreme Court's June 2009 decision to overturn her ruling in the New Haven fire department case. As the days passed by, however, the main focus of Republican opposition coalesced around a statement that Sotomayor made back in 2001. During a speech that year to Latino law students, she had made reference to a favorite saying of Sandra Day O'Connor and Ruth Bader Ginsberg, the first two female Supreme Court justices in U.S. history. After noting that O'Connor and Ginsberg were fond of stating that a "wise old woman" and a "wise old man" would come to the same conclusions, Sotomayor added that "I would hope that a wise Latina woman with the richness of her experiences would more often than not reach a better conclusion than a white male who hasn't lived that life."

Sotomayor's confirmation hearings before the Senate Judiciary Committee began on July 13, 2009. Over the next few days, Democratic Senators offered friendly questioning while Republican senators subjected her to intense cross-examination. The single greatest focus of Republican inquiry was her "wise Latina" comments of eight years before. Sotomayor tried to defuse the controversy by dismissing the statement as "a rhetorical flourish that fell flat." She explained that her statement was simply an effort "to inspire young Hispanics, Latino students, and lawyers to believe that their life experiences added value to the process." Finally, the judge tried to reassure skeptical Republicans by stating "unequivocally and without doubt: I do not believe that any ethnic, racial, or gender group has an advantage in sound judging."

As the questioning continued, Sotomayor remained calm and unruffled, reassuring the committee members that she would never let personal feelings influence her rulings. When the hearing was over, the committee voted 13-6 to endorse the nomination. On August 6, the full Senate voted in favor of Sotomayor's Supreme Court nomination by a 68-31 vote. When Obama

President Barack Obama and Vice President Joe Biden pose with Supreme Court justices prior to the investiture ceremony for Sotomayor, September 2009. From left: Associate Justices Samuel Alito, Ruth Bader Ginsburg, Anthony M. Kennedy, John Paul Stevens, Chief Justice John Roberts, President Obama, Associate Justice Sonia Sotomayor, Vice President Biden, Associate Justices Antonin Scalia, Clarence Thomas, Stephen Beyer, and retired Associate Justice David Souter.

heard the news, he declared that "this is a wonderful day for Judge Sotomayor and her family, but I also think it's a wonderful day for America."

Enjoying a Landmark Moment

Sotomayor was sworn into membership on the Supreme Court on August 8, 2009, at a ceremony led by Chief Justice John G. Roberts Jr. A few days later, at a White House reception organized to celebrate the event, she described her membership on the Court as "the most humbling honor of my life." But Sotomayor emphasized that her confirmation "would never have been possible without the opportunities presented to me by this nation.... I am struck again today by the wonder of my own life, and the life we in America are so privileged to lead."

Sotomayor also singled out her mother for special words of thanks. "I have often said that I am all I am because of her, and I am only half the woman she is." For her part, Celina expressed immense pride in her daughter. "I am proud of her, not because she is a Supreme Court justice, but because she is a good person," Celina said. "She has a big, beautiful, and kind heart."

Friends and supporters of Sotomayor say that her "big, beautiful, and kind heart" will also ensure that she keeps her promise to Obama to always remember her roots. This confidence seems well-placed. A few days after her confirmation, for example, she was the guest of honor at a lavish dinner held at the home of singer-actress Jennifer Lopez and her husband, music star Marc Anthony. At the conclusion of the dinner, which featured a menu of Puerto Rican delicacies, Sotomayor personally sought out all the cooks and staff responsible for preparing the meal. "I prepare fancy dinners all the time for dignitaries and stars, and never has this happened," said head chef Ricardo Cardona. "She showed us—all these Latino immigrants who were in the kitchen working to make the meal special—that she is one of us."

After being selected for the Court, Sotomayor called it "the most humbling honor of my life" and emphasized that it "would never have been possible without the opportunities presented to me by this nation.... I am struck again today by the wonder of my own life, and the life we in America are so privileged to lead."

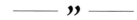

HOME AND FAMILY

Sotomayor married high school sweetheart Kevin Noonan in 1976, just before entering Yale Law School. They divorced in 1983 without having any children. She remains close to her mother, brother, and many of her nieces, nephews, and cousins.

HOBBIES AND OTHER INTERESTS

Sotomayor likes to cook, work out, and attend ballet and theatrical productions. She is also a big fan of the New York Yankees.

SELECTED HONORS AND AWARDS

Pyne Prize (Princeton University): 1976
Outstanding Latino Professional Award (Latino/a Law Students Association): 2006

FURTHER READING

Periodicals

Current Events, Sep. 7, 2009, p.4

Latina, Dec. 2009-Jan. 2010, p.108

National Review, June 22, 2009, p.28

New York, June 8, 2009, p.14

New York Times, Sep. 25, 1992; May 15, 2009, p.A21; May 27, 2009, p.A1; May 28, 2009, p.A16; June 5, 2009, p.A1; July 10, 2009, p.A1; July 15, 2009, p.A17; July 16, 2009, p. A18; Aug. 7, 2009, p.A1; Aug. 9, 2009, p.A12; Sep. 9, 2009, p.A12

New York Times Magazine, Nov. 27, 1983, p.118

Newsweek, July 20, 2009, p.43; Aug. 31, 2009, p.29

People, Aug. 17, 2009, p.75

Time, June 8, 2009, p.24; June 15, 2009, p.23; June 22, 2009, p.35

Time for Kids, Sep. 18, 2009, p.4

USA Today, July 15, 2009, p.A10; July 16, 2009, p. A4; July 17, 2009, p.A7; Aug. 10, 2009, p.A4

Online Articles

http://www.abanet.org/publiced/hispanic_s.htm
   (American Bar Association, "National Hispanic Heritage Month 2000, Profile—Week 4: Sonia Sotomayor," 2000)

http://www.dailyprincetonian.com/2009/05/13/23695
   (Daily Princetonian, "At Princeton, Sotomayor'76 Excelled at Academics, Extracurriculars," May 13, 2009)

http://www.law.com/jsp/nylj/PubArticleNY.jsp?id=1202430720254&slreturn=1&hbxlogin=1
   (New York Law Journal, "Sotomayor Is Pragmatic, Empathetic Lawyers Say," May 15, 2009)

http://topics.nytimes.com/top/reference/timestopics/people/s/sonia_sotomayor/index.html
   (New York Times, New York Times Topics: Sonia Sotomayor, n.d.)

http://thecaucus.blogs.nytimes.com/2009/09/25/sotomayor-offers-details-on-her-nomination
   (New York Times, "Sotomayor Offers Details on Her Nomination," Sep. 25, 2009)

http://www.washingtonpost.com/wp-dyn/content/article/2009/05/26/AR2009052600914.html
   (Washington Post, "Heritage Shapes Judge's Perspective," May 27, 2009)

ADDRESS

Sonia Sotomayor
U.S. Supreme Court
Supreme Court Bldg.
1 First Street NE
Washington, DC 20543

WORLD WIDE WEB SITES

http://www.oyez.org
http://www.supremecourtus.gov

Photo and Illustration Credits

Front Cover Photos: Charles Bolden: NASA; Stephenie Meyer: Ingo Wagner/dpa/Landov; Albert Pujols: AP Photo/Rob Carr, File; Sonia Sotomayor: Steve Petteway, Collection of the Supreme Court of the United States.

Charles Bolden/Photos: NASA/Bill Ingalls (p. 9); NASA (pp. 12, 14); NASA/Johnson Space Center (p. 16); NASA/Bill Ingalls (pp. 19, 20).

Robin Chase/Photos: © 2007 Tanit Sakakini (p. 25); Family photo, courtesy Robin Chase (p. 26); Courtesy Zipcar, Inc. (pp. 28, 30); © Stephen Oakley (p. 33).

Jesse James/Photos: TV still: JESSE JAMES IS A DEAD MAN/Spike TV (p. 37); PRNewsFoto via Newscom (p. 40); Courtesy of Discovery Channel/PRNewsFoto via Newscom (p. 42); AP Photo/Jean-Marc Bouju (p. 45); TV still: JESSE JAMES IS A DEAD MAN/Spike TV (p. 47).

Chuck Liddell/Photos: TV still: GUYS CHOICE AWARDS 2008/Spike TV (p. 51); Courtesy, Cal Poly Athletics Media Relations (p. 53); UPI Photo/Roger Williams via Newscom (p. 56); Francis Specker/Landov (p. 59); ABC/Adam Larkey (p. 61).

Mary Mary/Photos: UPI Photo/Arianne Teeple via Newscom (p. 65); Album cover: THANKFUL © 2000 Legacy/Columbia/Sony Music Entertainment (p. 68); Album cover: THE SOUND © 2008 Columbia/Sony Music Entertainment (p. 71); Jason Merritt/Getty Images (p. 73).

Stephenie Meyer/Photos: Ingo Wagner/dpa/Landov (p. 77); Book cover: TWILIGHT (Little, Brown and Company). Text copyright © 2005 by Stephenie Meyer. All rights reserved. Jacket design by Gail Doobinin. Jacket photo by Roger Hagadone. (p. 80); Movie still: TWILIGHT © Summit Entertainment, LLC. All rights reserved. (p. 83); Movie poster: NEW MOON © 2009 Summit Entertainment, LLC. All rights reserved. (p. 85); Movie still: ECLIPSE © 2010 Summit Entertainment, LLC. All rights reserved. Photo by Kimberley French. (p. 86); John Shearer/WireImage (p. 89).

Keke Palmer/Photos: PRNewsFoto/Nickelodeon via Newscom (p. 93); Movie still: TYLER PERRY'S MADEA'S FAMILY REUNION © 2006 Lions Gate Entertainment. All rights reserved. Photo by Alfeo Dixon. (p. 95); Movie still: AKEELAH AND THE BEE © 2006 Lions Gate Entertainment. All rights reserved. Photo by Saeed Adyani. (p. 97); Movie still: THE LONGSHOTS © 2008 The Weinstein Company. All rights reserved. Photo by Tony Rivetti Jr./Dimensions Films. (p. 99); AP Photo/Lisa Rose (p. 100).

Cumulative Names Index

This cumulative index includes the names of all individuals profiled in *Biography Today* since the debut of the series in 1992.

Aaliyah . . . . Jan 02
Aaron, Hank . . . . Sport V.1
Abbey, Edward . . . . WorLdr V.1
Abdul, Paula . . . . Jan 92
    Update 02
Abdul-Jabbar, Kareem . . . . Sport V.1
Abzug, Bella . . . . Sep 98
Adams, Ansel . . . . Artist V.1
Adams, William (will.i.am)
   see Black Eyed Peas . . . . Apr 06
Adams, Yolanda . . . . Apr 03
Adu, Freddy . . . . Sport V.12
Affleck, Ben . . . . Sep 99
Agassi, Andre . . . . Jul 92
Agosto, Ben . . . . Sport V.14
Aguilera, Christina . . . . Apr 00
Aidid, Mohammed Farah . . . . . WorLdr V.2
Aikman, Troy . . . . Apr 95;
    Update 01
Alba, Jessica . . . . Sep 01
Albright, Madeleine . . . . Apr 97
Alcindor, Lew
   see Abdul-Jabbar, Kareem . . . . . . Sport V.1
Aldrich, George . . . . Science V.11
Alexander, Elizabeth . . . . Apr 09
Alexander, Lloyd . . . . Author V.6
Alexander, Shaun . . . . Apr 07
Ali, Laila . . . . Sport V.11
Ali, Muhammad . . . . Sport V.2
Allen, Marcus . . . . Sep 97
Allen, Tim . . . . Apr 94;
    Update 99
Allen, Tori . . . . Sport V.9
Allen, Will . . . . Sep 09
Alley, Kirstie . . . . Jul 92
Almond, David . . . . Author V.10
Alvarez, Julia . . . . Author V.17
Alvarez, Luis W. . . . . Science V.3
Aly & AJ . . . . Sep 08
Amanpour, Christiane . . . . Jan 01

Amend, Bill . . . . Author V.18
Amin, Idi . . . . WorLdr V.2
Amman, Simon . . . . Sport V.8
An Na . . . . Author V.12
Anders, C.J.
   see Bennett, Cherie . . . . Author V.9
Anderson, Brett (Donna A.)
   see Donnas . . . . Apr 04
Anderson, Gillian . . . . Jan 97
Anderson, Laurie Halse . . . . . . Author V.11
Anderson, Marian . . . . Jan 94
Anderson, Terry . . . . Apr 92
André 3000
   see OutKast . . . . Sep 04
Andretti, Mario . . . . Sep 94
Andrews, Ned . . . . Sep 94
Angelou, Maya . . . . Apr 93
Aniston, Jennifer . . . . Apr 99
Annan, Kofi . . . . Jan 98
    Update 01
Anthony, Carmelo . . . . Sep 07
apl.de.ap (Alan Pineda Lindo)
   see Black Eyed Peas . . . . Apr 06
Applegate, K.A. . . . . Jan 00
Arafat, Yasir . . . . Sep 94
    Update 94; Update 95; Update 96;
    Update 97; Update 98; Update 00;
    Update 01; Update 02
Arantes do Nascimento, Edson
   see Pelé . . . . Sport V.1
Aristide, Jean-Bertrand . . . . Jan 95
    Update 01
Armstrong, Billie Joe
   see Green Day . . . . Apr 06
Armstrong, Lance . . . . Sep 00
    Update 00; Update 01; Update 02
Armstrong, Robb . . . . Author V.9
Armstrong, William H. . . . . Author V.7
Arnesen, Liv . . . . Author V.15
Arnold, Roseanne . . . . Oct 92
Asbaty, Diandra . . . . Sport V.14

Ashanti . . . . PerfArt V.2
Ashe, Arthur . . . . Sep 93
Ashley, Maurice . . . . Sep 99
Asimov, Isaac . . . . Jul 92
Askins, Renee . . . . WorLdr V.1
Attenborough, David . . . . Science V.4
Atwater-Rhodes, Amelia . . . . . . Author V.8
Aung San Suu Kyi . . . . Apr 96
    Update 98; Update 01; Update 02
Avi . . . . Jan 93
Babbitt, Bruce . . . . Jan 94
Babbitt, Natalie . . . . Jan 04
Baca, Judy . . . . Sep 09
Backstreet Boys . . . . Jan 00
Bahrke, Shannon . . . . Sport V.8
Bailey, Donovan . . . . Sport V.2
Baiul, Oksana . . . . Apr 95
Baker, James . . . . Oct 92
Baldwin, James . . . . Author V.2
Ballard, Robert . . . . Science V.4
Banda, Hastings Kamuzu . . . . WorLdr V.2
Banks, Tyra . . . . PerfArt V.2
Bardeen, John . . . . Science V.1
Barkley, Charles . . . . Apr 92
    Update 02
Barr, Roseanne
    see Arnold, Roseanne . . . . Oct 92
Barron, Robert . . . . Science V.9
Barrymore, Drew . . . . Jan 01
Barton, Hazel . . . . Science V.6
Basich, Tina . . . . Sport V.12
Bass, Bill . . . . Apr 08
Bass, Lance
    see *N Sync . . . . Jan 01
Bates, Daisy . . . . Apr 00
Battle, Kathleen . . . . Jan 93
Bauer, Joan . . . . Author V.10
Beachley, Layne . . . . Sport V.9
Bearden, Romare . . . . Artist V.1
Beckett, Josh . . . . Sport V.11
Beckham, David . . . . Jan 04
Belbin, Tanith . . . . Sport V.14
Bell, Drake . . . . Jan 07
Bell, Kristen . . . . Sep 05
Bellamy, Carol . . . . Jan 06
Bemelmans, Ludwig . . . . Author V.16
Ben-Ari, Miri . . . . Jan 06
Benjamin, André
    see OutKast . . . . Sep 04
Benjamin, Regina . . . . Science V.9
Bennett, Cherie . . . . Author V.9
Bennett, Olivia . . . . Sep 03

Bennington, Chester
    see Linkin Park . . . . Jan 04
Benson, Mildred . . . . Jan 03
Berenstain, Jan . . . . Author V.2
Berenstain, Stan . . . . Author V.2
Bergen, Candice . . . . Sep 93
Berger, Francie . . . . Sep 04
Berners-Lee, Tim . . . . Science V.7
Berry, Halle . . . . Jan 95
    Update 02
Bethe, Hans A. . . . . Science V.3
Beyoncé . . . . Jan 10
    see also Destiny's Child . . . . Apr 01
Bezos, Jeff . . . . Apr 01
Bhutto, Benazir . . . . Apr 95
    Update 99; Update 02
Bialik, Mayim . . . . Jan 94
Biden, Joe . . . . Sep 09
Big Boi
    see OutKast . . . . Sep 04
bin Laden, Osama . . . . Apr 02
Binford, Greta . . . . Jan 08
Bird, Larry . . . . Jan 92
    Update 98
Bird, Sue . . . . Sport V.9
Black, Jack . . . . Jan 05
Black, Thomas
    see Black, Jack . . . . Jan 05
Black Eyed Peas . . . . Apr 06
Blackmun, Harry . . . . Jan 00
Blair, Bonnie . . . . Apr 94
    Update 95
Blair, Tony . . . . Apr 04
Blake, James . . . . Sport V.14
Blanchard, Rachel . . . . Apr 97
Bledel, Alexis . . . . Jan 03
Bleiler, Gretchen . . . . Sport V.13
Blige, Mary J. . . . . Apr 02
Bloom, Orlando . . . . Sep 04
Bloor, Edward . . . . Author V.15
Blum, Deborah . . . . Science V.8
Blume, Judy . . . . Jan 92
Bolden, Charles . . . . Apr 10
Bonds, Barry . . . . Jan 03
Bono . . . . Sep 06
Booker, Cory . . . . Jan 08
Borgman, Jim . . . . Author V.15
Boulmerka, Hassiba . . . . Sport V.1
Bourdon, Rob
    see Linkin Park . . . . Jan 04
Bourke-White, Margaret . . . . Artist V.1

Boutros-Ghali, Boutros . . . . Apr 93
Update 98
Boyd, Candy Dawson . . . . Author V.3
Boyle, Ryan . . . . Sport V.10
Boyz II Men . . . . Jan 96
Bradbury, Ray . . . . Author V.3
Bradley, Ed . . . . Apr 94
Brady, Tom . . . . Sport V.7
Branch, Michelle . . . . PerfArt V.3
Brandis, Jonathan . . . . Sep 95
Brandy . . . . Apr 96
Brashares, Ann . . . . Author V.15
Breathed, Berke . . . . Jan 92
Breazeal, Cynthia . . . . Jan 09
Brin, Sergey . . . . Sep 05
Brody, Adam . . . . Sep 05
Brody, Jane . . . . Science V.2
Brooks, Garth . . . . Oct 92
Brooks, Gwendolyn . . . . Author V.3
Brooks, Vincent . . . . Sep 03
Brower, David . . . . WorLdr V.1
Update 01
Brown, Chris . . . . Apr 07
Brown, Claude . . . . Author V.12
Brown, Ron . . . . Sep 96
Bruchac, Joseph . . . . Author V.18
Brundtland, Gro Harlem . . . . . . Science V.3
Bryan, Zachery Ty . . . . Jan 97
Bryant, Kobe . . . . Apr 99
Buckley, Kelsie . . . . Sep 06
Buffett, Warren . . . . Business V.1
Burger, Warren . . . . Sep 95
Burke, Chris . . . . Sep 93
Burns, Ken . . . . Jan 95
Burnside, Aubyn . . . . Sep 02
Burrell, Stanley Kirk
see Hammer . . . . Jan 92
Bush, Barbara . . . . Jan 92
Bush, George . . . . Jan 92
Bush, George W. . . . . Sep 00
Update 00; Update 01; Update 02
Bush, Laura . . . . Apr 03
Bush, Sophia . . . . Apr 08
Butcher, Susan . . . . Sport V.1
Byars, Betsy . . . . Author V.4
Bynes, Amanda . . . . Sep 03
Cabot, Meg . . . . Author V.12
Calder, Alexander . . . . Artist V.1
Calderone, Mary S. . . . . Science V.3
Cameron, Candace . . . . Apr 95

Campbell, Erica
see Mary Mary . . . . Apr 10
Campbell, Neve . . . . Apr 98
Campbell, Tina
see Mary Mary . . . . Apr 10
Canady, Alexa . . . . Science V.6
Candy, John . . . . Sep 94
Cantore, Jim . . . . Science V.9
Caplan, Arthur . . . . Science V.6
Capolino, Peter . . . . Business V.1
Capriati, Jennifer . . . . Sport V.6
Card, Orson Scott . . . . Author V.14
Carey, Mariah . . . . Apr 96
Carle, Eric . . . . Author V.1
Carmona, Richard . . . . Science V.8
Carpenter, Mary Chapin . . . . Sep 94
Carrabba, Chris . . . . Apr 05
Carrey, Jim . . . . Apr 96
Carson, Ben . . . . Science V.4
Carson, Rachel . . . . WorLdr V.1
Carter, Aaron . . . . Sep 02
Carter, Chris . . . . Author V.4
Carter, Jimmy . . . . Apr 95
Update 02
Carter, Majora . . . . Sep 08
Carter, Nick
see Backstreet Boys . . . . Jan 00
Carter, Regina . . . . Sep 07
Carter, Vince . . . . Sport V.5
Update 01
Carvey, Dana . . . . Jan 93
Case, Steve . . . . Science V.5
Castellano, Torry (Donna C.)
see Donnas . . . . Apr 04
Castro, Fidel . . . . Jul 92
Update 94
Catchings, Tamika . . . . Sport V.14
Cera, Michael . . . . Apr 09
Chagall, Marc . . . . Artist V.1
Chamberlain, Wilt . . . . Sport V.4
Chambers, Veronica . . . . Author V.15
Champagne, Larry III . . . . Apr 96
Chan, Jackie . . . . PerfArt V.1
Chan Kwong Sang
see Chan, Jackie . . . . PerfArt V.1
Chase, Robin . . . . Apr 10
Chasez, JC
see *N Sync . . . . Jan 01
Chastain, Brandi . . . . Sport V.4
Update 00

For cumulative general, places of birth, and birthday indexes, please see biographytoday.com.

177

Chavez, Cesar . . . . Sep 93
Chavez, Julz . . . . Sep 02
Chavis, Benjamin . . . . Jan 94
    Update 94
Cheney, Dick . . . . Jan 02
Chihuly, Dale . . . . Jan 06
Childress, Alice . . . . Author V.1
Choldenko, Gennifer . . . . Author V.18
Christo . . . . Sep 96
Chung, Connie . . . . Jan 94
    Update 95; Update 96
Cisneros, Henry . . . . Sep 93
Clark, Kelly . . . . Sport V.8
Clarkson, Kelly . . . . Jan 03
Clay, Cassius Marcellus Jr.
    see Ali, Muhammad . . . . Sport V.2
Cleary, Beverly . . . . Apr 94
Clements, Andrew . . . . Author V.13
Clemons, Kortney . . . . Sep 07
Clijsters, Kim . . . . Apr 04
Clinton, Bill . . . . Jul 92
    Update 94; Update 95; Update 96; Update
    97; Update 98; Update 99; Update 00;
    Update 01
Clinton, Chelsea . . . . Apr 96
    Update 97; Update 01
Clinton, Hillary Rodham . . . Apr 93; Jan 10
    Update 94; Update 95; Update 96;
    Update 99; Update 00; Update 01
Cobain, Kurt . . . . Sep 94
Cohen, Adam Ezra . . . . Apr 97
Cohen, Sasha . . . . Sport V.12
Colfer, Eoin . . . . Author V.13
Collier, Bryan . . . . Author V.11
Collins, Billy . . . . Author V.16
Collins, Eileen . . . . Science V.4
Collins, Francis . . . . Science V.6
Combs, Benji
    see Madden, Benji . . . . PerfArt V.3
Combs, Joel
    see Madden, Joel . . . . PerfArt V.3
Combs, Sean (Puff Daddy) . . . . Apr 98
Cool, Tré (Frank Edwin Wright III)
    see Green Day . . . . Apr 06
Coolio . . . . Sep 96
Cooney, Barbara . . . . Author V.8
Cooney, Caroline B. . . . . Author V.4
Cooper, Anderson . . . . Sep 08
Cooper, Floyd . . . . Author V.17
Cooper, Susan . . . . Author V.17

Córdova, France . . . . Science V.7
Cormier, Robert . . . . Author V.1
    Update 01
Cosby, Bill . . . . Jan 92
Cosgrove, Miranda . . . . Jan 09
Coughlin, Natalie . . . . Sport V.10
Cousteau, Jacques . . . . Jan 93
    Update 97
Covel, Toby Keith
    see Keith, Toby . . . . Jan 05
Coville, Bruce . . . . Author V.9
Cox, Lynne . . . . Sport V.13
Crabtree, Taylor . . . . Jan 07
Crawford, Cindy . . . . Apr 93
Cray, Seymour . . . . Science V.2
Creech, Sharon . . . . Author V.5
Crichton, Michael . . . . Author V.5
Crilley, Mark . . . . Author V.15
Cronin, John . . . . WorLdr V.3
Crosby, Sidney . . . . Sport V.14
Cruz, Celia . . . . Apr 04
Culkin, Macaulay . . . . Sep 93
Culpepper, Daunte . . . . Sport V.13
Curtis, Christopher Paul . . . . Author V.4
    Update 00
Cushman, Karen . . . . Author V.5
Cyrus, Miley . . . . Sep 07
da Silva, Fabiola . . . . Sport V.9
Dae-jung, Kim
    see Kim Dae-jung . . . . Sep 01
Dahl, Roald . . . . Author V.1
Dai Qing . . . . WorLdr V.3
Dakides, Tara . . . . Sport V.7
Dalai Lama . . . . Sep 98
Daly, Carson . . . . Apr 00
Danes, Claire . . . . Sep 97
Daniel, Beth . . . . Sport V.1
Danziger, Paula . . . . Author V.6
Davenport, Lindsay . . . . Sport V.5
Davis, Jeremy
    see Paramore . . . . Apr 10
Davis, Jim . . . . Author V.1
Dawson, Matel Jr. . . . . Jan 04
Dayne, Ron . . . . Apr 00
de Klerk, F.W. . . . . Apr 94
    Update 94
de Mille, Agnes . . . . Jan 95
Delany, Bessie . . . . Sep 99
Delany, Sadie . . . . Sep 99
Dell, Michael . . . . Business V.1

Delson, Brad
  see Linkin Park . . . . Jan 04
DeMayo, Neda . . . . Apr 06
Denton, Sandi
  see Salt 'N' Pepa . . . . Apr 95
dePaola, Tomie . . . . Author V.5
Depp, Johnny . . . . Apr 05
Destiny's Child . . . . Apr 01
  see also Beyoncé . . . . Jan 10
Devers, Gail . . . . Sport V.2
Diana, Princess of Wales . . . . Jul 92
  Update 96; Update 97; Jan 98
Diaz, Cameron . . . . PerfArt V.3
DiCamillo, Kate . . . . Author V.10
DiCaprio, Leonardo . . . . Apr 98
Diemer, Walter . . . . Apr 98
Diesel, Vin . . . . Jan 03
Dion, Celine . . . . Sep 97
Dirnt, Mike (Michael Pritchard)
  see Green Day . . . . Apr 06
Dixie Chicks . . . . PerfArt V.1
Doherty, Shannen . . . . Apr 92
  Update 94
Dole, Bob . . . . Jan 96
  Update 96
Dole, Elizabeth . . . . Jul 92
  Update 96; Update 99
Domingo, Placido . . . . Sep 95
Donnas . . . . Apr 04
Donovan, Marion . . . . Science V.9
Dorough, Howie
  see Backstreet Boys . . . . Jan 00
Douglas, Marjory Stoneman . . WorLdr V.1;
  Update 98
Dove, Rita . . . . Jan 94
Dragila, Stacy . . . . Sport V.6
Draper, Sharon . . . . Apr 99
Driscoll, Jean . . . . Sep 97
Duchovny, David . . . . Apr 96
Duff, Hilary . . . . Sep 02
Duke, David . . . . Apr 92
Dumars, Joe . . . . Sport V.3
  Update 99
Dumitriu, Ioana . . . . Science V.3
Dunbar, Paul Lawrence . . . . Author V.8
Duncan, Lois . . . . Sep 93
Duncan, Tim . . . . Apr 04
Dunlap, Alison . . . . Sport V.7
Dunst, Kirsten . . . . PerfArt V.1
Dworkin, Aaron . . . . Apr 07

Earle, Sylvia . . . . Science V.1
Earnhardt, Dale . . . . Apr 01
Earnhardt, Dale Jr. . . . . Sport V.12
Ebadi, Shirin . . . . Apr 04
Edelman, Marian Wright . . . . Apr 93
Efron, Zac . . . . Apr 08
Egozy, Eran . . . . Jan 10
Elion, Getrude . . . . Science V.6
Ellerbee, Linda . . . . Apr 94
Elliott, Missy . . . . PerfArt V.3
Ellison, Ralph . . . . Author V.3
Elway, John . . . . Sport V.2
  Update 99
Eminem . . . . Apr 03
Engelbart, Douglas . . . . Science V.5
Erdös, Paul . . . . Science V.2
Estefan, Gloria . . . . Jul 92
Evans, Janet . . . . Jan 95
  Update 96
Eve . . . . Jan 05
Evert, Chris . . . . Sport V.1
Ewing, Patrick . . . . Jan 95
  Update 02
Fall Out Boy . . . . Sep 07
Fanning, Dakota . . . . Jan 06
Fanning, Shawn . . . . Science V.5
  Update 02
Farmer, Nancy . . . . Author V.6
Farmer, Paul Jr. . . . . Science V.11
Farrakhan, Louis . . . . Jan 97
Farrell, Dave
  see Linkin Park . . . . Jan 04
Farrell, Suzanne . . . . PerfArt V.1
Farro, Josh
  see Paramore . . . . Apr 10
Farro, Zac
  see Paramore . . . . Apr 10
Fatone, Joey
  see *N Sync . . . . Jan 01
Fauci, Anthony S. . . . . Science V.7
Favre, Brett . . . . Sport V.2
Fay, Michael . . . . Science V.9
Federer, Roger . . . . Jan 07
Fedorov, Sergei . . . . Apr 94
  Update 94
Feelings, Tom . . . . Author V.16
Felix, Allyson . . . . Sport V.10
Fenty, Robyn Rihanna
  see Rihanna . . . . Apr 08
Fergie (Ferguson, Stacy)
  see Black Eyed Peas . . . . Apr 06

Ferguson, Stacy (Fergie)
see Black Eyed Peas . . . . Apr 06
Fernandez, Lisa . . . . Sport V.5
Ferrell, Will . . . . Apr 07
Ferrera, America . . . . Sep 07
Fey, Tina . . . . Author V.16
Feynman, Richard P. . . . . Science V.10
Fiasco, Lupe . . . . Sep 09
Ficker, Roberta Sue
see Farrell, Suzanne . . . . PerfArt V.1
Fielder, Cecil . . . . Sep 93
Fields, Debbi . . . . Jan 96
Filipovic, Zlata . . . . Sep 94
Finch, Jennie . . . . Jan 05
Fiorina, Carly . . . . Sep 01
Update 01; Update 02
Fitzgerald, Ella . . . . Jan 97
Fitzhugh, Louise . . . . Author V.3
Flake, Sharon . . . . Author V.13
Flannery, Sarah . . . . Science V.5
Flowers, Vonetta . . . . Sport V.8
Foray, June . . . . Jan 07
Ford, Cheryl . . . . Sport V.11
Ford, Harrison . . . . Sep 97
Ford, Maya (Donna F.)
see Donnas . . . . Apr 04
Foreman, Dave . . . . WorLdr V.1
Forman, James . . . . Apr 05
Forman, Michele . . . . Jan 03
Fossey, Dian . . . . Science V.1
Foudy, Julie . . . . Sport V.13
Fox, Paula . . . . Author V.15
Fox, Vicente . . . . Apr 03
Frank, Anne . . . . Author V.4
Frankenthaler, Helen . . . . Artist V.1
Franklin, Aretha . . . . Apr 01
Freedman, Russell . . . . Author V.14
Freeman, Cathy . . . . Jan 01
Fresh Prince
see Smith, Will . . . . Sep 94
Friday, Dallas . . . . Sport V.10
Fu Mingxia . . . . Sport V.5
Fuentes, Daisy . . . . Jan 94
Fuller, Millard . . . . Apr 03
Funk, Mary Wallace
see Funk, Wally . . . . Jan 05
Funk, Wally . . . . Jan 05
Funke, Cornelia . . . . Sep 05
Gaiman, Neil . . . . Jan 10
Galdikas, Biruté . . . . Science V.4
Galeczka, Chris . . . . Apr 96

Gantos, Jack . . . . Author V.10
Garcia, Jerry . . . . Jan 96
Garcia, Sergio . . . . Sport V.7
Garnett, Kevin . . . . Sport V.6
Garth, Jennie . . . . Apr 96
Gates, Bill . . . . Apr 93
Update 98; Update 00; Science V.5;
Update 01
Gates, Henry Louis Jr. . . . . Apr 00
Gayle, Helene . . . . Science V.8
Geisel, Theodor Seuss
see Seuss, Dr. . . . . Jan 92
Gellar, Sarah Michelle . . . . Jan 99
George, Eddie . . . . Sport V.6
George, Jean Craighead . . . . Author V.3
Gerberding, Julie . . . . Science V.10
Gibbs, Lois . . . . WorLdr V.1
Giddens, Rebecca . . . . Sport V.14
Giff, Patricia Reilly . . . . Author V.7
Giguère, Jean-Sébastien . . . . Sport V.10
Gilbert, Sara . . . . Apr 93
Gilbert Stoga, Gloria
see Stoga, Gloria Gilbert . . . . Sep 09
Gilbert, Walter . . . . Science V.2
Gillespie, Dizzy . . . . Apr 93
Gilman, Billy . . . . Apr 02
Gingrich, Newt . . . . Apr 95
Update 99
Ginsburg, Ruth Bader . . . . Jan 94
Giuliani, Rudolph . . . . Sep 02
Glenn, John . . . . Jan 99
Glennie, Evelyn . . . . PerfArt V.3
Glover, Savion . . . . Apr 99
Goldberg, Whoopi . . . . Apr 94
Gomez, Jamie (Taboo)
see Black Eyed Peas . . . . Apr 06
Gomez, Selena . . . . Sep 08
Gonzalez, Tony . . . . Sport V.11
Good Charlotte
see Madden, Benji and
Madden, Joel . . . . PerfArt V.3
Goodall, Jane . . . . Science V.1
Update 02
Goodman, John . . . . Sep 95
Gorbachev, Mikhail . . . . Jan 92
Update 96
Gordon, Jeff . . . . Apr 99
Gore, Al . . . . Jan 93; Sep 08
Gorey, Edward . . . . Author V.13

For cumulative general, places of birth, and birthday indexes, please see biographytoday.com.

Gould, Stephen Jay .... Science V.2;
  Update 02
Graf, Steffi .... Jan 92
  Update 01
Granato, Cammi .... Sport V.8
Grandberry, Omari Ishmael
  see Omarion .... Jan 09
Grandin, Temple .... Science V.3
GrandPré, Mary .... Author V.14
Granny D
  see Haddock, Doris. .... Sep 00
Grant, Amy .... Jan 95
Graves, Earl .... Business V.1
Green Day .... Apr 06
Greenburg, Dan .... Author V.14
Greer, Pedro José Jr.. .... Science V.10
Gretzky, Wayne .... Jan 92
  Update 93; Update 99
Griese, Brian .... Jan 02
Griffey, Ken Jr. .... Sport V.1
Griffith Joyner, Florence .... Sport V.1
  Update 98
Grimes, Nikki. .... Author V.14
Grisham, John. .... Author V.1
Groening, Matt .... Jan 92
Groppe, Laura .... Science V.5
Guey, Wendy .... Sep 96
Guisewite, Cathy .... Sep 93
Gumbel, Bryant .... Apr 97
Guy, Jasmine .... Sep 93
Guy, Rosa .... Author V.9
Gwaltney, John Langston ..... Science V.3
Gyatso, Tenzin
  see Dalai Lama .... Sep 98
Haddix, Margaret Peterson ... Author V.11
Haddock, Doris. .... Sep 00
Hahn, Joe
  see Linkin Park. .... Jan 04
Haile Selassie .... WorLdr V.2
Hakim, Joy .... Author V.16
Halaby, Lisa
  see Noor al Hussein, Queen
    of Jordan .... Jan 05
Hale, Shannon .... Author V.18
Haley, Alex .... Apr 92
Hamilton, Bethany .... Apr 05
Hamilton, Laird .... Sport V.13
Hamilton, Virginia .... Author V.1;
  Author V.12
Hamm, Mia. .... Sport V.2
  Update 00

Hammer .... Jan 92
Hampton, David .... Apr 99
Handford, Martin. .... Jan 92
Handler, Daniel
  see Snicket, Lemony .... Author V.12
Handler, Ruth. .... Apr 98
  Update 02
Hanh, Thich Nhat
  see Nhat Hanh (Thich) .... Jan 04
Hanks, Tom .... Jan 96
Hansberry, Lorraine .... Author V.5
Hanson .... Jan 98
Hanson, Ike
  see Hanson .... Jan 98
Hanson, Taylor
  see Hanson .... Jan 98
Hanson, Zac
  see Hanson .... Jan 98
Harbaugh, Jim .... Sport V.3
Hardaway, Anfernee "Penny" ... Sport V.2
Harding, Tonya .... Sep 94
Hargreaves, Alison. .... Jan 96
Harris, Bernard. .... Science V.3
Harrison, James .... Sep 09
Hart, Melissa Joan .... Jan 94
Hartnett, Josh .... Sep 03
Hasek, Dominik .... Sport V.3
Hassan II .... WorLdr V.2
  Update 99
Hathaway, Anne .... Apr 05
Haughton, Aaliyah Dana
  see Aaliyah .... Jan 02
Hawk, Tony. .... Apr 01
Hawking, Stephen. .... Apr 92
Hayden, Carla .... Sep 04
Hayes, Tyrone . ... Science V.10
Haynes, Cornell Jr.
  see Nelly .... Sep 03
Healy, Bernadine .... Science V.1
  Update 01
Heimlich, Henry .... Science V.6
Heinlein, Robert. .... Author V.4
Hendrickson, Sue .... Science V.7
Henry, Marguerite .... Author V.4
Hernandez, Livan .... Apr 98
Herriot, James .... Author V.1
Hesse, Karen .... Author V.5
  Update 02
Hewitt, Jennifer Love. .... Sep 00
Hewson, Paul
  see Bono .... Sep 06

For cumulative general, places of birth, and birthday indexes, please see biographytoday.com.

181

Hiaasen, Carl . . . . Author V.18
Highmore, Freddie . . . . Apr 06
Hill, Anita . . . . Jan 93
Hill, Faith . . . . Sep 01
Hill, Grant . . . . Sport V.1
Hill, Lauryn . . . . Sep 99
Hillary, Sir Edmund . . . . Sep 96
Hillenbrand, Laura . . . . Author V.14
Hillenburg, Stephen . . . . Author V.14
Hingis, Martina . . . . Sport V.2
Hinton, S.E. . . . . Author V.1
Ho, David . . . . Science V.6
Hobbs, Will . . . . Author V.18
Hogan, Hulk . . . . Apr 92
Holdsclaw, Chamique . . . . Sep 00
Holmes, Katie . . . . Jan 00
Holmes, Priest . . . . Apr 05
Honoré, Russel . . . . Jan 06
Hooper, Geoff . . . . Jan 94
Hopper, Grace Murray . . . . Science V.5
Horner, Jack . . . . Science V.1
Horvath, Polly . . . . Author V.16
Hoskins, Michele . . . . Business V.1
House, Donna . . . . Science V.11
Houston, Whitney . . . . Sep 94
Howard, Tim . . . . Apr 06
Howe, Gordie . . . . Sport V.2
Howe, James . . . . Author V.17
Hrdy, Sarah Blaffer . . . . Apr 07
Hudgens, Vanessa . . . . Jan 08
Hudson, Jennifer . . . . Jan 08
Huerta, Dolores . . . . Sep 03
Hughes, Langston . . . . Author V.7
Hughes, Sarah . . . . Jan 03
Hunter, Zach . . . . Jan 08
Hunter-Gault, Charlayne . . . . Jan 00
Hurley, Andy
    see Fall Out Boy . . . . Sep 07
Hurston, Zora Neale . . . . Author V.6
Hussein, King . . . . Apr 99
Hussein, Saddam . . . . Jul 92
    Update 96; Update 01; Update 02
Iacocca, Lee A. . . . . Jan 92
Ice-T . . . . Apr 93
Iglesias, Enrique . . . . Jan 03
Irwin, Bindi . . . . Apr 08
Irwin, Steve . . . . Science V.7
Iverson, Allen . . . . Sport V.7
Ivey, Artis Jr.
    see Coolio . . . . Sep 96
Jackman, Hugh . . . . Jan 10

Jackson, Bo . . . . Jan 92
    Update 93
Jackson, Jesse . . . . Sep 95
    Update 01
Jackson, Peter . . . . PerfArt V.2
Jackson, Phil . . . . Sport V.10
Jackson, Shirley . . . . Author V.6
Jackson, Shirley Ann . . . . Science V.2
Jaco, Wasalu Muhammad
    see Fiasco, Lupe . . . . Sep 09
Jacobs, Christianne Meneses
    see Meneses Jacobs, Christianne . . . . Jan 10
Jacques, Brian . . . . Author V.5
Jaffurs, Lee Wardlaw
    see Wardlaw, Lee . . . . Sep 08
Jagr, Jaromir . . . . Sport V.5
Jakes, T.D. . . . . Jan 05
James, Cheryl
    see Salt 'N' Pepa . . . . Apr 95
James, Jesse . . . . Apr 10
James, LeBron . . . . Sport V.12
Jamison, Judith . . . . Jan 96
Jansen, Dan . . . . Apr 94
Javacheff, Christo V.
    see Christo . . . . Sep 96
Jeffers, Eve
    see Eve . . . . Jan 05
Jemison, Mae . . . . Oct 92
Jenkins, Jerry B. . . . . Author V.16
Jennings, Peter . . . . Jul 92
Jeter, Derek . . . . Sport V.4
Jewel . . . . Sep 98
Jiménez, Francisco . . . . Author V.13
Jobs, Steven . . . . Jan 92; Science V.5
John Paul II . . . . Oct 92
    Update 94; Update 95; Sep 05
Johns, Jasper . . . . Artist V.1
Johnson, Angela . . . . Author V.6
Johnson, Jimmie . . . . Sep 09
Johnson, Jimmy . . . . Jan 98
Johnson, Johanna . . . . Apr 00
Johnson, John . . . . Jan 97
Johnson, Keyshawn . . . . Sport V.10
Johnson, Lonnie . . . . Science V.4
Johnson, Magic . . . . Apr 92
    Update 02
Johnson, Michael . . . . Jan 97
    Update 00
Johnson, Randy . . . . Sport V.9
Johnston, Lynn . . . . Jan 99

Jonas, Joseph
see Jonas Brothers . . . . Jan 08
Jonas, Kevin
see Jonas Brothers . . . . Jan 08
Jonas, Nick
see Jonas Brothers . . . . Jan 08
Jonas Brothers . . . . Jan 08
Jones, Chuck . . . . Author V.12
Jones, Diana Wynne . . . . Author V.15
Jones, James Earl . . . . Jan 95
Jones, Marion . . . . Sport V.5
Jones, Norah . . . . PerfArt V.2
Jones, Quincy . . . . PerfArt V.2
Jordan, Barbara . . . . Apr 96
Jordan, Michael . . . . Jan 92
Update 93; Update 94; Update 95;
Update 99; Update 01
Joy, Bill . . . . Science V.10
Joyner-Kersee, Jackie . . . . Oct 92
Update 96; Update 97; Update 98
Jung, Kim Dae
see Kim Dae-jung . . . . Sep 01
Juster, Norton . . . . Author V.14
Ka Hsaw Wa . . . . WorLdr V.3
Kaddafi, Muammar
see Qaddafi, Muammar . . . . Apr 97
Kadohata, Cynthia . . . . Sep 06
Kamen, Dean . . . . Science V.11
Kamler, Kenneth . . . . Science V.6
Kapell, Dave . . . . Science V.8
Kaunda, Kenneth . . . . WorLdr V.2
Keene, Carolyne
see Benson, Mildred . . . . Jan 03
Keith, Toby . . . . Jan 05
Kenyatta, Jomo . . . . WorLdr V.2
Kenyon, Cynthia . . . . Science V.11
Kerr, M.E. . . . . Author V.1
Kerrigan, Nancy . . . . Apr 94
Keys, Alicia . . . . Jan 07
Kidd, Jason . . . . Sport V.9
Kielburger, Craig . . . . Jan 00
Kiessling, Laura L. . . . . Science V.9
Kilcher, Jewel
see Jewel . . . . Sep 98
Kimball, Cheyenne . . . . Jan 07
Kim Dae-jung . . . . Sep 01
King, Coretta Scott . . . . Sep 06
King, Mary-Claire . . . . Science V.10
King, Stephen . . . . Author V.1
Update 00
Kiraly, Karch . . . . Sport V.4

Kirkpatrick, Chris
see *N Sync . . . . Jan 01
Kistler, Darci . . . . Jan 93
Klug, Chris . . . . Sport V.8
Klum, Heidi . . . . Apr 09
Knightley, Keira . . . . Apr 07
Knowles, Beyoncé
see Beyoncé . . . . Jan 10
see Destiny's Child . . . . Apr 01
Koff, Clea . . . . Science V.11
Konigsburg, E.L. . . . . Author V.3
Kopp, Wendy . . . . Sep 07
Krakauer, Jon . . . . Author V.6
Kratt, Chris . . . . Science V.10
Kratt, Martin . . . . Science V.10
Krauss, Alison . . . . Apr 05
Krim, Mathilde . . . . Science V.1
Krone, Julie . . . . Jan 95
Update 00
Kübler-Ross, Elisabeth . . . . Science V.10
Kurzweil, Raymond . . . . Science V.2
Kutcher, Ashton . . . . Apr 04
Kwan, Michelle . . . . Sport V.3
Update 02
Kwolek, Stephanie . . . . Science V.10
Laden, Osama bin
see bin Laden, Osama . . . . Apr 02
LaDuke, Winona . . . . WorLdr V.3
Update 00
LaHaye, Tim . . . . Author V.16
Lalas, Alexi . . . . Sep 94
Lama, Dalai
see Dalai Lama . . . . Sep 98
Land, Edwin . . . . Science V.1
lang, k.d. . . . . Sep 93
Lang Lang . . . . Apr 09
Lansky, Bruce . . . . Author V.17
Larson, Gary . . . . Author V.1
Lasky, Kathryn . . . . Author V.18
Lasseter, John . . . . Sep 00
Lavigne, Avril . . . . PerfArt V.2
Lawrence, Jacob . . . . Artist V.1
Update 01
Leakey, Louis . . . . Science V.1
Leakey, Mary . . . . Science V.1
Lee, Harper . . . . Author V.9
Lee, Jeanette . . . . Apr 03
Lee, Spike . . . . Apr 92
Lee, Stan . . . . Author V.7
Update 02
Le Guin, Ursula K. . . . . Author V.8

Leibovitz, Annie .... Sep 96
Lemelson, Jerome .... Science V.3
Lemieux, Mario .... Jul 92
  Update 93
LeMond, Greg .... Sport V.1
L'Engle, Madeleine......... Jan 92; Apr 01
Lennox, Betty .... Sport V.13
Leno, Jay .... Jul 92
Leopold, Aldo .... WorLdr V.3
Leslie, Lisa .... Jan 04
Lester, Julius .... Author V.7
Letterman, David .... Jan 95
Levi-Montalcini, Rita .... Science V.1
Levine, Gail Carson.......... Author V.17
Lewis, C.S..................... Author V.3
Lewis, Carl...................... Sep 96
  Update 97
Lewis, John....................... Jan 03
Lewis, Leona .... Apr 09
Lewis, Shari .... Jan 99
Liddell, Chuck................... Apr 10
Lidstrom, Nicklas .... Sep 03
Lil' Romeo
  see Romeo, Lil'.................. Jan 06
Limbaugh, Rush .... Sep 95
  Update 02
Lin, Maya........................ Sep 97
Lindgren, Astrid............. Author V.13
Lindo, Alan Pineda (apl.de.ap)
  see Black Eyed Peas .... Apr 06
Ling, Lisa....................... Apr 08
Linkin Park .... Jan 04
Lionni, Leo.................... Author V.6
Lipinski, Tara .... Apr 98
Lipsyte, Robert .... Author V.12
Lisanti, Mariangela .... Sep 01
Littrell, Brian
  see Backstreet Boys .... Jan 00
Liukin, Nastia .... Jan 09
Lobel, Arnold .... Author V.18
Lobo, Rebecca .... Sport V.3
Locklear, Heather............... Jan 95
Lohan, Lindsay .... Sep 04
Long, Irene D. .... Jan 04
Lopez, Charlotte................. Apr 94
López, George................ PerfArt V.2
Lopez, Jennifer .... Jan 02
Lovato, Demi .... Sep 09
Love, Susan.................... Science V.3
Lovell, Jim .... Jan 96

Lowe, Alex .... Sport V.4
Lowman, Meg................. Science V.4
Lowry, Lois .... Author V.4
Lucas, George.................... Apr 97
  Update 02
Lucid, Shannon .... Science V.2
Lynch, Chris .... Author V.13
Ma, Yo-Yo .... Jul 92
Maathai, Wangari ..... WorLdr V.1; Sep 05
Mac, Bernie .... PerfArt V.1
MacArthur, Ellen.............. Sport V.11
Macaulay, David .... Author V.2
MacLachlan, Patricia .... Author V.2
Madden, Benji .... PerfArt V.3
Madden, Joel................. PerfArt V.3
Madden, John.................... Sep 97
Maddux, Greg .... Sport V.3
Maguire, Martie
  see Dixie Chicks............. PerfArt V.1
Maines, Natalie
  see Dixie Chicks............. PerfArt V.1
Mallett, Jef .... Apr 09
Mandela, Nelson .... Jan 92
  Update 94; Update 01
Mandela, Winnie .... WorLdr V.2
Mangel, Marcel
  see Marceau, Marcel .... PerfArt V.2
Mankiller, Wilma .... Apr 94
Manning, Eli..................... Sep 08
Manning, Peyton. .... Sep 00
Mantle, Mickey.................... Jan 96
Marceau, Marcel.............. PerfArt V.2
Margulis, Lynn................... Sep 96
Marino, Dan .... Apr 93
  Update 00
Marrow, Tracy
  see Ice-T...................... Apr 93
Mars, Forrest Sr.............. Science V.4
Marsalis, Wynton .... Apr 92
Marshall, Thurgood............... Jan 92
  Update 93
Martin, Ann M................... Jan 92
Martin, Bernard............. WorLdr V.3
Martin, Ricky.................... Jan 00
Martinez, Pedro................. Sport V.5
Martinez, Victor .... Author V.15
Mary Mary .... Apr 10
Masih, Iqbal.................... Jan 96
Mathers, Marshall III
  see Eminem .... Apr 03
Mathis, Clint................... Apr 03

Mathison, Melissa . . . . Author V.4
Maxwell, Jody-Anne . . . . Sep 98
Mayer, John . . . . Apr 04
McAdams, Rachel . . . . Apr 06
McCain, John . . . . Apr 00
McCarty, Oseola . . . . Jan 99
    Update 99
McCary, Michael
    see Boyz II Men . . . . Jan 96
McClintock, Barbara . . . . Oct 92
McCloskey, Robert . . . . Author V.15
McCully, Emily Arnold . . . . Jul 92
    Update 93
McDaniel, Lurlene . . . . Author V.14
McDonald, Janet . . . . Author V.18
McEntire, Reba . . . . Sep 95
McGrady, Tracy . . . . Sport V.11
McGrath, Judy . . . . Business V.1
McGruder, Aaron . . . . Author V.10
McGwire, Mark . . . . Jan 99
    Update 99
McKissack, Fredrick L. . . . . Author V.3
McKissack, Patricia C. . . . . Author V.3
McLean, A.J.
    see Backstreet Boys . . . . Jan 00
McNabb, Donovan . . . . Apr 03
McNair, Steve . . . . Sport V.11
McNutt, Marcia . . . . Science V.11
Mead, Margaret . . . . Science V.2
Meaker, Marijane
    see Kerr, M.E. . . . . Author V.1
Mebarak Ripoll, Shakira Isabel
    see Shakira . . . . PerfArt V.1
Meissner, Kimmie . . . . Sep 08
Meltzer, Milton . . . . Author V.11
Memmel, Chellsie . . . . Sport V.14
Menchu, Rigoberta . . . . Jan 93
Mendes, Chico . . . . WorLdr V.1
Meneses Jacobs, Christianne . . . . . . Jan 10
Messier, Mark . . . . Apr 96
Meyer, Stephenie . . . . Apr 10
Michalka, Alyson Renae
    see Aly & AJ . . . . Sep 08
Michalka, Amanda Joy
    see Aly & AJ . . . . Sep 08
Milbrett, Tiffeny . . . . Sport V.10
Millan, Cesar . . . . Sep 06
Miller, Percy Romeo
    see Romeo, Lil' . . . . Jan 06
Miller, Rand . . . . Science V.5

Miller, Robyn . . . . Science V.5
Miller, Shannon . . . . Sep 94
    Update 96
Milosevic, Slobodan . . . . Sep 99
    Update 00; Update 01; Update 02
Mirra, Dave . . . . Sep 02
Mister Rogers
    see Rogers, Fred . . . . PerfArt V.3
Mitchell-Raptakis, Karen . . . . Jan 05
Mittermeier, Russell A. . . . . WorLdr V.1
Miyamoto, Shigeru . . . . Science V.5
Mobutu Sese Seko . . . . WorLdr V.2;
    Update 97
Moceanu, Dominique . . . . Jan 98
Mohajer, Dineh . . . . Jan 02
Mohammed, Warith Deen . . . . Apr 09
Monroe, Bill . . . . Sep 97
Montana, Joe . . . . Jan 95
    Update 95
Moore, Henry . . . . Artist V.1
Moore, Mandy . . . . Jan 04
Moreno, Arturo R. . . . . Business V.1
Morgan, Garrett . . . . Science V.2
Morissette, Alanis . . . . Apr 97
Morita, Akio . . . . Science V.4
Morris, Nathan
    see Boyz II Men . . . . Jan 96
Morris, Wanya
    see Boyz II Men . . . . Jan 96
Morrison, Lillian . . . . Author V.12
Morrison, Samuel . . . . Sep 97
Morrison, Toni . . . . Jan 94
Moseley, Jonny . . . . Sport V.8
Moses, Grandma . . . . Artist V.1
Moss, Cynthia . . . . WorLdr V.3
Moss, Randy . . . . Sport V.4
Mother Teresa
    see Teresa, Mother . . . . Apr 98
Mowat, Farley . . . . Author V.8
Mugabe, Robert . . . . WorLdr V.2
Muhammad, Wallace Delaney
    see Mohammed, Warith Dean . . . . Apr 09
Muir, John . . . . WorLdr V.3
Mulanovich, Sofia . . . . Apr 07
Muldowney, Shirley . . . . Sport V.7
Muniz, Frankie . . . . Jan 01
Murie, Margaret . . . . WorLdr V.1
Murie, Olaus J. . . . . WorLdr V.1
Murphy, Eddie . . . . PerfArt V.2
Murphy, Jim . . . . Author V.17

Murray, Ty . . . . Sport V.7
Myers, Mike . . . . PerfArt V.3
Myers, Walter Dean . . . . Jan 93
    Update 94; Jan 09
Myers, Walter Milton
    see Myers, Walter Dean . . . . Jan 09
*N Sync . . . . Jan 01
Nakamura, Leanne . . . . Apr 02
Napoli, Donna Jo . . . . Author V.16
Nash, John Forbes Jr. . . . . Science V.7
Nash, Steve. Jan 06
Navratilova, Martina . . . . Jan 93
    Update 94
Naylor, Phyllis Reynolds. . . . . Apr 93
Ndeti, Cosmas . . . . Sep 95
Nechita, Alexandra. . . . . Jan 98
Nelly. . . . . Sep 03
Nelson, Gaylord . . . . WorLdr V.3
Nelson, Marilyn . . . . Author V.13
Nevelson, Louise. . . . . Artist V.1
Newman, Ryan . . . . Sport V.11
Newsom, Lee Ann. . . . . Science V.11
Nhat Hanh (Thich) . . . . Jan 04
Nicklaus, Jack . . . . Sport V.2
Niedermayer, Scott. . . . . Jan 08
Nielsen, Jerri. . . . . Science V.7
Nixon, Joan Lowery. . . . . Author V.1
Nixon, Richard . . . . Sep 94
Nkrumah, Kwame . . . . WorLdr V.2
Noor al Hussein, Queen of Jordan . . Jan 05
Norman, Christina. . . . . Apr 08
Norman, Greg . . . . Jan 94
Norwood, Brandy
    see Brandy . . . . Apr 96
Novello, Antonia. . . . . Apr 92
    Update 93
Nureyev, Rudolf . . . . Apr 93
Nye, Bill. Science V.2
Nye, Naomi Shihab. . . . . Author V.8
Nyerere, Julius Kambarage . . . WorLdr V.2;
    Update 99
Obama, Barack . . . . Jan 07
Obama, Michelle . . . . Sep 09
O'Brien, Soledad. . . . . Jan 07
Ocampo, Adriana C. . . . . Science V.8
Ochoa, Ellen . . . . Apr 01
    Update 02
Ochoa, Lorena . . . . Sport V.14
Ochoa, Severo . . . . Jan 94
O'Connor, Sandra Day. . . . . Jul 92

O'Dell, Scott . . . . Author V.2
O'Donnell, Rosie. . . . . Apr 97
    Update 02
Ohno, Apolo. . . . . Sport V.8
Oka, Masi. . . . . Jan 08
O'Keeffe, Georgia. . . . . Artist V.1
Olajuwon, Hakeem. . . . . Sep 95
Oleynik, Larisa. . . . . Sep 96
Oliver, Jamie. . . . . Apr 07
Oliver, Patsy Ruth . . . . WorLdr V.1
Olsen, Ashley . . . . Sep 95
Olsen, Mary Kate. . . . . Sep 95
Omarion . . . . Jan 09
O'Neal, Shaquille . . . . Sep 93
Opdyke, Irene Gut . . . . Author V.9
Oppenheimer, J. Robert. . . . . . . Science V.1
Orman, Suze. . . . . Apr 09
Ortega, Kenny. . . . . Jan 09
Otto, Sylke . . . . Sport V.8
OutKast . . . . Sep 04
Ovechkin, Alexander. . . . . Jan 10
Page, Larry. . . . . Sep 05
Paisley, Brad. . . . . Jan 10
Pak, Se Ri . . . . Sport V.4
Palenik, Skip . . . . Jan 07
Palmer, Keke . . . . Apr 10
Palmer, Violet. . . . . Sep 05
Paolini, Christopher. . . . . Author V.16
Paramore . . . . Apr 10
Park, Linda Sue . . . . Author V.12
Park, Nick . . . . Sep 06
Parker, Candace . . . . Jan 10
Parkinson, Jennifer. . . . . Apr 95
Parks, Gordon . . . . Artist V.1
Parks, Rosa . . . . Apr 92
    Update 94; Apr 06
Pascal, Francine . . . . Author V.6
Paterson, Katherine . . . . Author V.3
Patrick, Danica. . . . . Apr 06
Patrick, Ruth. . . . . Science V.3
Patterson, Carly . . . . Sport V.12
Patterson, Ryan . . . . Science V.7
Pattinson, Robert . . . . Sep 09
Patton, Antwan
    see OutKast . . . . Sep 04
Paul, Chris . . . . Apr 09
Pauley, Jane. . . . . Oct 92
Pauling, Linus . . . . Jan 95
Paulsen, Gary . . . . Author V.1
Payton, Walter . . . . Jan 00

For cumulative general, places of birth, and birthday indexes, please see biographytoday.com

Pearman, Raven-Symone
see Raven . . . . Apr 04
Peck, Richard . . . . Author V.10
Peet, Bill . . . . Author V.4
Pei, I.M. . . . . Artist V.1
Pelé . . . . Sport V.1
Pelosi, Nancy . . . . Sep 07
Perlman, Itzhak . . . . Jan 95
Perot, H. Ross . . . . Apr 92
Update 93; Update 95; Update 96
Perry, Luke . . . . Jan 92
Perry, Tyler . . . . Sep 08
Peterson, Roger Tory . . . . WorLdr V.1
Petty, Richard . . . . Sport V.2
Phelps, Michael . . . . Sport V.13; Jan 09
Phoenix, River . . . . Apr 94
Pierce, Tamora . . . . Author V.13
Pike, Christopher . . . . Sep 96
Pine, Elizabeth Michele . . . . Jan 94
Pinkney, Andrea Davis . . . . Author V.10
Pinkney, Jerry . . . . Author V.2
Pinkwater, Daniel . . . . Author V.8
Pinsky, Robert . . . . Author V.7
Pippen, Scottie . . . . Oct 92
Pippig, Uta . . . . Sport V.1
Pitt, Brad . . . . Sep 98
Portman, Natalie . . . . Sep 99
Potter, Beatrix . . . . Author V.8
Poussaint, Alvin . . . . Science V.9
Powell, Colin . . . . Jan 92
Update 93; Update 95; Update 01
Prelutsky, Jack . . . . Author V.2; Sep 07
Pressel, Morgan . . . . Jan 08
Priestley, Jason . . . . Apr 92
Prinze, Freddie Jr. . . . . Apr 00
Pritchard, Michael (Mike Dirnt)
see Green Day . . . . Apr 06
Probst, Jeff . . . . Jan 01
Protess, David . . . . Apr 10
Puff Daddy
see Combs, Sean (Puff Daddy) . . . . . Apr 98
Puffy
see Combs, Sean (Puff Daddy) . . . . . Apr 98
Pujols, Albert . . . . Sport V.12; Apr 10
Pullman, Philip . . . . Author V.9
Qaddafi, Muammar . . . . Apr 97
Qing, Dai
see Dai Qing . . . . WorLdr V.3
Queen Latifah . . . . Apr 92
Quesada, Vicente Fox
see Fox, Vicente . . . . Apr 03

Quintanilla, Selena
see Selena . . . . Jan 96
Rabin, Yitzhak . . . . Oct 92
Update 93; Update 94; Update 95
Radcliffe, Daniel . . . . Jan 02
Ramirez, Manny . . . . Sport V.13
Ramos, Jorge . . . . Apr 06
Raven . . . . Apr 04
Ray, Rachael . . . . Apr 09
Raymond, Usher IV
see Usher . . . . PerfArt V.1
Reagan, Ronald . . . . Sep 04
Reeve, Christopher . . . . Jan 97
Update 02
Reeves, Keanu . . . . Jan 04
Reid Banks, Lynne . . . . Author V.2
Rennison, Louise . . . . Author V.10
Reno, Janet . . . . Sep 93
Update 98
Rice, Anne . . . . Author V.3
Rice, Condoleezza . . . . Apr 02
Rice, Jerry . . . . Apr 93
Richardson, Dot . . . . Sport V.2
Update 00
Richardson, Kevin
see Backstreet Boys . . . . Jan 00
Ride, Sally . . . . Jan 92
Rigopulos, Alex . . . . Jan 10
Rihanna . . . . Apr 08
Riley, Dawn . . . . Sport V.4
Rimes, LeAnn . . . . Jan 98
Rinaldi, Ann . . . . Author V.8
Ringgold, Faith . . . . Author V.2
Ripken, Cal Jr. . . . . Sport V.1
Update 01
Risca, Viviana . . . . Sep 00
Rivera, Diego . . . . Artist V.1
Roba, Fatuma . . . . Sport V.3
Roberts, Cokie . . . . Apr 95
Roberts, Emma . . . . Apr 09
Roberts, John Jr. . . . . Apr 08
Roberts, Julia . . . . Sep 01
Roberts, Robin . . . . Jan 09
Robertson, Allison (Donna R.)
see Donnas . . . . Apr 04
Robinson, David . . . . Sep 96
Robinson, Jackie . . . . Sport V.3
Robinson, Mary . . . . Sep 93
Robison, Emily
see Dixie Chicks . . . . PerfArt V.1
Rockwell, Norman . . . . Artist V.1

Roddick, Andy . . . . Jan 03
Rodman, Dennis . . . . Apr 96
    Update 99
Rodriguez, Alex. . . . . Sport V.6
Rodriguez, Eloy . . . . Science V.2
Rodriguez, Gloria . . . . Apr 05
Rodriguez, Ivan "Pudge" . . . . Jan 07
Roethlisberger, Ben. . . . . Sep 06
Rogers, Fred. . . . . PerfArt V.3
Romeo, Lil' . . . . Jan 06
Romero, John . . . . Science V.8
Roper, Dee Dee
    see Salt 'N' Pepa . . . . Apr 95
Rosa, Emily . . . . Sep 98
Rose, Pete . . . . Jan 92
Rosenberger, Grayson. . . . . Jan 09
Rowan, Carl . . . . Sep 01
Rowland, Kelly
    see Destiny's Child . . . . Apr 01
Rowland, Pleasant T. . . . . Business V.1
Rowling, J.K. . . . . Sep 99
    Update 00; Update 01; Update 02; Jan 08
Roy, Patrick . . . . Sport V.7
Rubin, Jamie. . . . . Science V.8
Rudolph, Wilma . . . . Apr 95
Runyan, Marla . . . . Apr 02
Russell, Charlie . . . . Science V.11
Ryan, Nolan . . . . Oct 92
    Update 93
Ryan, Pam Muñoz . . . . Author V.12
Ryder, Winona . . . . Jan 93
Rylant, Cynthia. . . . . Author V.1
Sabin, Albert. . . . . Science V.1
Sachar, Louis. . . . . Author V.6
Sacks, Oliver. . . . . Science V.3
Sadat, Anwar . . . . WorLdr V.2
Safina, Dinara . . . . Apr 09
Sagan, Carl . . . . Science V.1
Salinger, J.D.. . . . . Author V.2
Salk, Jonas . . . . Jan 94
    Update 95
Salt 'N' Pepa . . . . Apr 95
Sampras, Pete . . . . Jan 97
    Update 02
Sanborn, Ryne. . . . . Sport V.8
Sanchez, Ricardo . . . . Sep 04
Sanchez Vicario, Arantxa . . . . Sport V.1
Sanders, Barry . . . . Sep 95
    Update 99

Sanders, Deion . . . . Sport V.1
Sandler, Adam. . . . . Jan 06
Santana, Carlos. . . . . Sep 05
Sapp, Warren . . . . Sport V.5
Saro-Wiwa, Ken . . . . WorLdr V.1
Satcher, David . . . . Sep 98
Savimbi, Jonas . . . . WorLdr V.2
Scalia, Antonin . . . . Jan 05
Scarry, Richard. . . . . Sep 94
Schilling, Curt . . . . Sep 05
Schroeder, Pat . . . . Jan 97
Schulz, Charles M . . . . Author V.2
    Update 00
Schwarzkopf, H. Norman. . . . . Jan 92
Schwikert, Tasha. . . . . Sport V.7
Scieszka, Jon. . . . . Author V.9
Scott, Jerry . . . . Author V.15
Scurry, Briana . . . . Jan 00
Sealfon, Rebecca . . . . Sep 97
Seinfeld, Jerry. . . . . Oct 92
    Update 98
Selena . . . . Jan 96
Seles, Monica. . . . . Jan 96
Sendak, Maurice. . . . . Author V.2
Senghor, Léopold Sédar . . . . . . WorLdr V.2
Sessions, Michael . . . . Apr 07
Seuss, Dr.. . . . . Jan 92
Shabazz, Betty . . . . Apr 98
Shakira. PerfArt V.1
Shakur, Tupac . . . . Apr 97
Sharapova, Maria. . . . . Sep 05
Shatner, William . . . . Apr 95
Shea, Jim Jr. . . . . Sport V.8
Shinoda, Mike
    see Linkin Park. . . . . Jan 04
Shula, Don . . . . Apr 96
Silva, Fabiola da
    see da Silva, Fabiola . . . . Sport V.9
Silverstein, Shel . . . . Author V.3
    Update 99
Simmons, Russell . . . . Apr 06
Simmons, Ruth . . . . Sep 02
Simpson, Ashlee . . . . Sep 05
Sinatra, Frank . . . . Jan 99
Singh, Vijay . . . . Sport V.13
Siskel, Gene . . . . Sep 99
Sleator, William . . . . Author V.11
Small, David . . . . Author V.10
Smith, Betty. . . . . Author V.17
Smith, Emmitt . . . . Sep 94

Smith, Will . . . . Sep 94
Smyers, Karen . . . . Sport V.4
Snicket, Lemony . . . . Author V.12
Snyder, Zilpha Keatley . . . . Author V.17
Sones, Sonya . . . . Author V.11
Soren, Tabitha . . . . Jan 97
Sorenstam, Annika . . . . Sport V.6
Soriano, Alfonso . . . . Sport V.10
Sosa, Sammy . . . . Jan 99
    Update 99
Soto, Gary . . . . Author V.5
Sotomayor, Sonia . . . . Apr 10
Spade, Kate . . . . Apr 07
Speare, Elizabeth George . . . . Sep 95
Spears, Britney . . . . Jan 01
Spears, Jamie Lynn . . . . Sep 06
Spelke, Elizabeth . . . . Science V.10
Spelman, Lucy . . . . Science V.6
Spencer, Diana
    see Diana, Princess of Wales . . . . Jul 92
    Update 96; Update 97; Jan 98
Spiegelman, Art . . . . Author V.17
Spielberg, Steven . . . . Jan 94
    Update 94; Update 95
Spinelli, Jerry . . . . Apr 93
Spock, Dr. Benjamin . . . . Sep 95
    Update 98
Stachowski, Richie . . . . Science V.3
Stanford, John . . . . Sep 99
Stefani, Gwen . . . . Sep 03
Steinem, Gloria . . . . Oct 92
Steingraber, Sandra . . . . Science V.9
Stern, Isaac . . . . PerfArt V.1
Stewart, James Jr. . . . . Apr 08
Stewart, Jon . . . . Jan 06
Stewart, Kordell . . . . Sep 98
Stewart, Kristen . . . . Jan 10
Stewart, Martha . . . . Business V.1
Stewart, Patrick . . . . Jan 94
Stewart, Tony . . . . Sport V.9
Stiles, Jackie . . . . Sport V.6
Stiles, Julia . . . . PerfArt V.2
Stine, R.L. . . . . Apr 94
Stockman, Shawn
    see Boyz II Men . . . . Jan 96
Stockton, John . . . . Sport V.3
Stoga, Gloria Gilbert . . . . Sep 09
Stoker, Joscelyn
    see Stone, Joss . . . . Jan 06
Stone, Joss . . . . Jan 06

Strahan, Michael . . . . Sport V.12
Strasser, Todd . . . . Author V.7
Street, Picabo . . . . Sport V.3
Streeter, Tanya . . . . Sport V.11
Strug, Kerri . . . . Sep 96
Stump, Patrick
    see Fall Out Boy . . . . Sep 07
Summitt, Pat . . . . Sport V.3
Suzuki, Ichiro . . . . Apr 08
Suzuki, Shinichi . . . . Sep 98
Swanson, Janese . . . . Science V.4
Swift, Taylor . . . . Jan 09
Swoopes, Sheryl . . . . Sport V.2
Taboo (Jamie Gomez)
    see Black Eyed Peas . . . . Apr 06
Tan, Amy . . . . Author V.9
Tandy, Karen P. . . . . Jan 08
Tarbox, Katie . . . . Author V.10
Tartakovsky, Genndy . . . . Author V.11
Tarter, Jill . . . . Science V.8
Tarvin, Herbert . . . . Apr 97
Taurasi, Diana . . . . Sport V.10
Taylor, Mildred D. . . . . Author V.1;
    Update 02
Taymor, Julie . . . . PerfArt V.1
Teller, Edward . . . . Science V.9
Tenberken, Sabriye . . . . Sep 07
Tenzin Gyatso
    see Dalai Lama . . . . Sep 98
Teresa, Mother . . . . Apr 98
Teter, Hannah . . . . Sep 06
Thampy, George . . . . Sep 00
Tharp, Twyla . . . . PerfArt V.3
Thich Nhat Hahn
    see Nhat Hanh (Thich) . . . . Jan 04
Thiessen, Tiffani-Amber . . . . Jan 96
Thomas, Clarence . . . . Jan 92
Thomas, Dave . . . . Apr 96
    Update 02
Thomas, Jonathan Taylor . . . . Apr 95
Thomas, Lewis . . . . Apr 94
Thomas, Rob . . . . Jan 07
Thompson, Jenny . . . . Sport V.5
Tienda, Marta . . . . Sep 08
Timberlake, Justin
    see *N Sync . . . . Jan 01
Timberlake, Justin . . . . Sep 08
Tisdale, Ashley . . . . Jan 07
Tolan, Stephanie S. . . . . Author V.14
Tolkien, J.R.R. . . . . Jan 02

Tomlinson, LaDainian......... Sport V.14
Tompkins, Douglas .... WorLdr V.3
Toro, Natalia..................... Sep 99
Torvalds, Linus .... Science V.11
Travers, P.L................... Author V.2
Tré Cool (Frank Edwin Wright III)
    see Green Day................... Apr 06
Trohman, Joe
    see Fall Out Boy.................. Sep 07
Trump, Donald .... Apr 05
Tubman, William V.S......... WorLdr V.2
Tucker, Chris..................... Jan 01
Tuttle, Merlin.................... Apr 97
Twain, Shania .... Apr 99
Tyson, Neil deGrasse .... Science V.11
Uchida, Mitsuko .... Apr 99
Underwood, Carrie .... Apr 07
Urlacher, Brian .... Sep 04
Usher .... PerfArt V.1
Van Allsburg, Chris .... Apr 92
Van Draanen, Wendelin...... Author V.11
Van Dyken, Amy..... Sport V.3; Update 00
Van Meter, Vicki .... Jan 95
Vasan, Nina .... Science V.7
Vega, Alexa .... Jan 04
Ventura, Jesse.................... Apr 99
    Update 02
Vernon, Mike .... Jan 98
    Update 02
Vick, Michael.................. Sport V.9
Vidal, Christina .... PerfArt V.1
Villa, Brenda .... Jan 06
Villa-Komaroff, Lydia .... Science V.6
Vincent, Mark
    see Diesel, Vin .... Jan 03
Voigt, Cynthia .... Oct 92
Vonnegut, Kurt Jr. .... Author V.1
Wa, Ka Hsaw
    see Ka Hsaw Wa.............. WorLdr V.3
Wade, Dwyane................. Sport V.14
Wadhwa, Meenakshi .... Science V.11
Wallace, Ben .... Jan 05
Walsh, Kerri .... Sport V.13
Walters, Barbara................. Sep 94
Wang, An..................... Science V.2
Ward, Charlie .... Apr 94
Ward, Lloyd D. .... Jan 01
Wardlaw, Lee .... Sep 08
Warhol, Andy.................. Artist V.1
Warner, Kurt..................... Sport V.4

Warrick, Earl................. Science V.8
Washington, Denzel .... Jan 93
    Update 02
Watley, Natasha............... Sport V.11
Watson, Barry .... Sep 02
Watson, Emma .... Apr 03
Watson, James D............. Science V.1
Watson, Paul .... WorLdr V.1
Watterson, Bill.................... Jan 92
Wayans, Keenen Ivory .... Jan 93
Weatherspoon, Teresa .... Sport V.12
Webb, Alan .... Sep 01
Webb, Karrie .... Sport V.5
    Update 01; Update 02
Weinke, Chris.................... Apr 01
Welling, Tom .... PerfArt V.3
Wentz, Pete
    see Fall Out Boy.................. Sep 07
Werbach, Adam .... WorLdr V.1
Whedon, Joss .... Author V.9
White, E.B...................... Author V.1
White, Jaleel...................... Jan 96
White, Reggie .... Jan 98
White, Ruth .... Author V.11
White, Shaun .... Sport V.14
Whitestone, Heather............. Apr 95
    Update 02
Whitman, Meg .... Sep 03
Whitson, Peggy .... Science V.9
Wie, Michelle .... Sep 04
Wilder, Laura Ingalls.......... Author V.3
WilderBrathwaite, Gloria ..... Science V.7
Wiles, Deborah............. Author V.18
will.i.am (William Adams)
    see Black Eyed Peas .... Apr 06
Williams, Garth .... Author V.2
Williams, Hayley
    see Paramore .... Apr 10
Williams, Lori Aurelia........ Author V.16
Williams, Michelle
    see Destiny's Child............... Apr 01
Williams, Robin.................. Apr 92
Williams, Serena .... Sport V.4
    Update 00; Update 02
Williams, Ted.................. Sport V.9
Williams, Tyler James .... Sep 06
Williams, Venus .... Jan 99
    Update 00; Update 01; Update 02
Williamson, Kevin............ Author V.6
Willingham, Tyrone .... Sep 02

 For cumulative general, places of birth, and birthday indexes, please see biographytoday.com

Wilson, August . . . . Author V.4
Wilson, Edward O. . . . . Science V.8
Wilson, Gretchen . . . . Sep 06
Wilson, Mara . . . . Jan 97
Winans, CeCe . . . . Apr 00
Winfield, Dave . . . . Jan 93
Winfrey, Oprah . . . . Apr 92
    Update 00; Business V.1
Winslet, Kate . . . . Sep 98
Witherspoon, Reese . . . . Apr 03
Wojtyla, Karol Josef
    see John Paul II . . . . Oct 92
    Update 94; Update 95
Wolf, Hazel . . . . WorLdr V.3
Wolff, Virginia Euwer . . . . Author V.13
Wood, Elijah . . . . Apr 02
Woodley, Shailene . . . . Sep 09
Woods, Tiger . . . . Sport V.1
    Update 00; Sport V.6
Woodson, Jacqueline . . . . Author V.7
    Update 01
Woo-Ping, Yuen
    see Yuen Wo-Ping . . . . PerfArt V.3
Wo-Ping, Yuen
    see Yuen Wo-Ping . . . . PerfArt V.3
Wortis, Avi
    see Avi . . . . Jan 93

Wozniak, Steve . . . . Science V.5
Wrede, Patricia C. . . . . Author V.7
Wright, Frank Edwin III (Tré Cool)
    see Green Day . . . . Apr 06
Wright, Frank Lloyd . . . . Artist V.1
Wright, Richard . . . . Author V.5
Wright, Will . . . . Apr 04
Yamaguchi, Kristi . . . . Apr 92
Yao Ming . . . . Sep 03
Yelas, Jay . . . . Sport V.9
Yeltsin, Boris . . . . Apr 92
    Update 93; Update 95; Update 96; Update
    98; Update 00
Yep, Laurence . . . . Author V.5
Yolen, Jane . . . . Author V.7
York, Taylor
    see Paramore . . . . Apr 10
Young, Steve . . . . Jan 94
    Update 00
Yuen Wo-Ping . . . . PerfArt V.3
Yunus, Muhammad . . . . Sep 07
Yzerman, Steve . . . . Sport V.2
Zamora, Pedro . . . . Apr 95
Zindel, Paul . . . . Author V.1
    Update 02
Zirkle, Aliy . . . . Sport V.6
Zmeskal, Kim . . . . Jan 94

Biography Today

General Series

For ages 9 and above

Biography Today **General Series** includes a unique combination of current biographical profiles that teachers and librarians — and the readers themselves — tell us are most appealing. The **General Series** is available as a 3-issue subscription; hardcover annual cumulation; or subscription plus cumulation.

Within the **General Series**, your readers will find a variety of sketches about:

- Authors
- Cartoonists
- Musicians
- Scientists
- Political leaders
- Astronauts
- Sports figures
- TV personalities
- Movie actresses & actors
- and the movers & shakers in many other fields!

ONE-YEAR SUBSCRIPTION

- 3 softcover issues, 6" x 9"
- Published in January, April, and September
- 1-year subscription, list price $66. **School and library price $64**
- 150 pages per issue
- 10 profiles per issue
- Contact sources for additional information
- Cumulative Names Index

HARDBOUND ANNUAL CUMULATION

- Sturdy 6" x 9" hardbound volume
- Published in December
- List price $73. **School and library price $66 per volume**
- 450 pages per volume
- 30 profiles — includes all profiles found in softcover issues for that calendar year
- Cumulative General Index, Places of Birth Index, and Birthday Index

SUBSCRIPTION AND CUMULATION COMBINATION

- $110 for 3 softcover issues plus the hardbound volume

For Cumulative General, Places of Birth, and Birthday Indexes, please see www.biographytoday.com.

"Biography Today will be useful in elementary and middle school libraries and in public library children's collections where there is a need for biographies of current personalities. High schools serving reluctant readers may also want to consider a subscription."
— *Booklist,* American Library Association

"Highly recommended for the young adult audience. Readers will delight in the accessible, energetic, tell-all style; teachers, librarians, and parents will welcome the clever format [and] intelligent and informative text. It should prove especially useful in motivating 'reluctant' readers or literate nonreaders."
— *MultiCultural Review*

"Written in a friendly, almost chatty tone, the profiles offer quick, objective information. While coverage of current figures makes *Biography Today* a useful reference tool, an appealing format and wide scope make it a fun resource to browse." — *School Library Journal*

"The best source for current information at a level kids can understand."
— Kelly Bryant, School Librarian, Carlton, OR

"Easy for kids to read. We love it! Don't want to be without it."
— Lynn McWhirter, School Librarian, Rockford, IL